Rajni Bakshi is a journalist, author, speaker and the founder of the YouTube channel, *Ahimsa Conversations*. Her books include *Bapu Kuti: Journeys in Rediscovery of Gandhi* (1998) and *Bazaars, Conversations and Freedom: For a Market Culture Beyond Greed and Fear* (2009), among others. Born in Delhi, she is currently based in Mumbai.

Vivekananda and Our Times

The Journey from
Fear to Love

Rajni Bakshi

TIGERBACKS | Speaking Tiger Short Non-Fiction

SPEAKING TIGER BOOKS LLP
125A, Ground Floor, Shahpur Jat, near Asiad Village,
New Delhi 110049

'A Hundred Years After Swami Vivekananda's Chicago Address' and
'The Dispute Over Swami Vivekananda's Legacy: A Warning and an
Opportunity' first published by Other India Press, Goa in 1993
This revised edition published by Speaking Tiger Books in 2024
'A Personal Reflection: Wherefore Now?' first published by
Speaking Tiger Books 2024

ISBN: 978-93-5447-727-0
eISBN: 978-93-5447-725-6

10 9 8 7 6 5 4 3 2 1

In memoriam
Anand Bapat
and
Darryl D'Monte

Contents

Introduction

On 11th September 1893, an unprecedented gathering took place on the shores of the ocean-like Lake Michigan in North America. Representatives of many of the world's religions met for several days on a shared platform. Diverse religions have intersected in both conflict and camaraderie for centuries. But the Parliament of World Religions, held at Chicago, was perhaps the first time in history that so many religions met on a formal platform in the spirit of inter-faith dialogue.

Like many Indians, I had a vague idea that it was at this event in Chicago that Swami Vivekananda came into the limelight. It was only in early 1993, as the centenary of Swamiji's Chicago address approached, that I became fascinated by his persona for two reasons. The first reason was born out of restless curiosity. How and why did Vivekananda so confidently assert that conflict between religions is utterly futile? The second reason was grief over the tragic irony that in Vivekananda's homeland, the centenary year of the Chicago address was marked by bitter conflict and brutal violence between Hindus and Muslims.

On 6th December 1992, thousands of supporters of the Ramjanmabhoomi campaign stormed and demolished the 16th century structure of the Babri Masjid. In response to this event there was a spate of brutally violent clashes between Hindus and Muslims in many parts of India. In Mumbai, where I lived, the violence subsided after a few days only to erupt again in January, taking on far more ferocious forms. Just as the city limped back to some semblance of normalcy, on 12th March 1993, there were powerful bomb blasts at 12 locations in Mumbai. An estimated 900 people had been killed in the December-January violence and another 257 were killed by the bomb blasts. Thousands more were injured, many of them handicapped for life.

Like many of my peers I was in a state of shell-shock. Along with friends and colleagues I participated in peace marches and joined a human-chain, called 'Harmony Across Bombay', in which ordinary people held hands in a line that stretched across some 43 kilometres. I have a vivid memory of joining the human chain at Parel, holding hands on one side with an elderly Parsi woman and on the other side with a school girl who had accompanied her entire class to this event.

Such actions felt good in that moment but they did not help to overcome a deep sense of foreboding. It was self-evident that with the demolition in Ayodhya and the violence of the following months—Indian politics and society had moved to a more complex level. The future began to look more grim and troubled than ever before.

This was the context in which I went looking for the text of Swami Vivekananda's speeches at the Parliament of World Religions in Chicago. I was struck by the poignancy of the fact that the audience at the Parliament of World Religions rose to its feet in a standing ovation on hearing just the first five words of Vivekananda's address—'Sisters and Brothers of America'.

What followed was, to begin with, a purely journalistic exercise. Sometime in April 1993 I went to the Resident Editor of *The Times of India* in Mumbai with a proposal for an 18-part series on Swami Vivekananda's journey to the gathering in Chicago in 1893. From the day that Swamiji sailed out of Bombay harbour to his first speech at the Parliament, there were 17 weeks. I proposed an 18-part series, after all, there would be need for a wrap-up article.

The Resident Editor then was Darryl D'Monte, who had been one of my mentors for well over a decade. Since he knew me well, Darryl smiled indulgently and laughed kindly as he said, 'You must be crazy to ask for an 18-part series.' But the story is so rich, so full of adventure and excitement—I appealed.

I had gone to Darryl with a detailed plan of how every article would be pegged on where Vivekananda was in that week a hundred years ago. Along with this geographical peg, each week's article would describe the historical context and spiritual quest that was taking Vivekananda to America and why this was relevant for us a hundred years later.

The relevance of such a series of articles in the centenary year of the Chicago address was self-evident. As editor, Darryl's challenge lay in deciding how much column space he could allocate to the idea. I offered to reduce the series by half, to nine articles.

'Only six,' Darryl said firmly, and I immediately agreed.

And so, starting on 30th May 1993—approximately a hundred years from when Vivekananda sailed out of Bombay harbour—the six part series began to appear in the *Sunday Review*, *The Times of India's* weekend magazine. The final article was published on 26th September 1993.

~

As I delved deeper into the *Collected Works of Swami Vivekananda*, this six-part series moved beyond being only a 'project' or just another piece of journalism. Reading Swamiji's letters and lectures became a sanctuary—one that felt like a fox-hole in a combat zone. As I read about the wide variety of situations and experiences which Vivekananda journeyed through, I began to see him as a friend, rather than as some remote persona on a pedestal. And as Swamiji led me to the life and teachings of Sri Ramakrishna Paramahamsa—deep gratitude overcame all other feelings.

I did start out in the spirit of countering the efforts

of those who deployed fragments of Vivekananda's writing to justify and promote communal animosity. But somewhere along the way this ceased to be the driving motivation. It became far more important to share what I had learnt about the struggles and triumphs of a rare man's life—a deeply self-aware man who located himself in a cosmic frame.

It was in this spirit that I shared my journeys with Swamiji at a seminar held at the Institute for Development Studies (IDS), Jaipur, in August 1993. The six articles published in the *Sunday Review* and an essay based on the paper I presented at the IDS seminar were together published by The Other India Press, Mapusa, Goa, in 1994.

Over the last 30 years Swamiji's presence has enriched my life in countless ways. He left this material world more than half a century before I was born but Vivekananda is a friend—for there are shared joys, disagreements and an enduring affinity on core values. It is not that I have often gone back to his writings. Yet through these three decades, Swamiji has been a constant inspiration—a cooling shade amid the searing turmoil of our times. After all, this turmoil is not just manifest in large events 'outside' in politics, society and public life at large. It has entered our daily life through bitter divisions among family and friends.

To be divided about the material approach to a particular problem can be creative—that wider variety of approaches can lead to a better solution. But when the division is between justifying hatred versus advocating compassion then the very basis of samaj/society is at stake.

From time to time I have been asked: What would Vivekananda do, or Gandhi do, in this situation? On principle I refuse to address this question. There are no possible answers to this question which can escape being presumptuous. What I do feel confident in sharing is an account of my own journey, through these troubled times, with the torch light of inspiration I draw from Vivekananda. This is what the concluding essay of this volume aims to do.

Why yet another book on Vivekananda? After all, over the last 30 years, there has been a wide variety of new writing on Vivekananda. The Ramakrishna Mission remains the single most prolific source of publications—including Vivekananda's own writings as well as biographies and commentaries by devotees and admirers. Independent, non-hagiographic biographies and commentaries have also multiplied. Many of these have grappled with the same question that struck me back in 1993—how and why is Vivekananda an inspiration both for those who seek communal harmony and those who are driven by communal animosity.

This book is meant for readers who want a brief and accessible account of Swamiji's ideas and strivings. It is particularly addressed to those who are disturbed by the cultural and moral crisis of our times and maybe curious about if and how Swamiji's journey can inspire and guide us today.

While I do not have a comprehensive knowledge of the wide array of new literature on Swamiji, I must mention two recent books that have contributed richly to a better understanding of Swamiji's universe and thus can inform our current struggles and strivings—*Vivekananda: The Philosopher of Freedom* by Govind Krishnan V. and *Swami Vivekananda's Vedāntic Cosmopolitanism* by Swami Medhananda.

Krishnan's book may have been intended as polemic—its sub-title is 'How the Sangh Parivar's Greatest Icon Is Its Arch Nemesis'. There is indeed plenty of polemical argumentation in this book but that pales in significance as Krishnan leads us through a rich account not only of Vivekananda's intellectual, moral and political strivings but also the context of the late 19th century in India, the USA and Europe.

In the process Krishnan has thrown a liberating light on several issues of contemporary relevance. For instance, he documents how Vivekananda treated with indifference the prohibition on Hindus eating beef. For Vivekananda, the taboo against eating beef was a cultural custom not something that was essential or core to Hinduism. Krishnan tells the story of how the worship of Goddess Uma in the form of a girl child, is usually done by worshiping an upper-caste Hindu girl.

But while in Srinagar, Vivekananda chose the four year old daughter of his Muslim boatman for this puja.

As a social and intellectual history, *The Philosopher of Freedom* paints a detailed picture of the extent to which, in the late 19th century, Hindus and India were misrepresented by the West—as being '...savage, pagan, sensual, barbarous, idolatrous, effeminate, irrational and primitive in contrast to the civilized, rational, masculine, and scientific West.'[1] Much of this 'othering' was a part and parcel of the Christian bigotry of that time.[2] The importance of Krishnan's narrative lies in both his starkly describing the nature of this bigotry and also the creative ways in which Vivekananda responded to it without being either defensive or becoming mired in a counter-bigotry. Krishnan's account is sufficiently detailed to also include those Western voices that condemned '...the bigoted and barbaric utterances of many Christian speakers, at the Parliament of World Religions.'[3]

On the whole, Krishnan's work is important for once again highlighting the danger of taking any one line or passage out of the totality of Vivekananda's journey and using the quote for a pre-determined purpose.

Medhananda's book is intended for people with a deep, even technical, interest in philosophy. He begins by conveying the essence of Vivekananda's life and teachings through this quote:

'Truth is my God, the universe my country.'[4]

Medhananda's motivation is to challenge a long line of scholars who have depicted Vivekananda as a colonial subject whose views were mainly a reaction to Western hegemony and the British occupation of India. Some Western scholars have labelled Vivekananda, Sri Aurobindo and Sarvepalli Radhakrishnan as 'Neo-Hindus' who disguised essentially Western ideas and values in superficially Indian garb in order to promote Indian nationalism. Medhananda challenges this as a falsehood by showing in great detail, how Vivekananda's Vedantic ethics was inspired by his guru Sri Ramakrishna Paramahamsa and not as a 'reaction' to the West.

Medhananda, who is a monk of the Ramakrishna Mission, responds to the need for reverential immersion in one's own indigenous tradition and thinking in our own concepts.[5] While this particular book is primarily concerned with details of philosophical traditions, in the process of setting the stage for this, Medhananda highlights Vivekananda's view that it was India's lack of openness to other cultures that was one of the main reasons for its protracted 'slavery' at the hands of Muslim and British rulers. Medhananda quotes Swamiji as follows:

'To become broad, to go out, to amalgamate, to universalise, is the end of our aims. ...With all my love for India, and with all my patriotism and veneration for the ancients, I cannot but think that we have to learn many things from other nations. We must be always ready to sit at the feet of all, for, mark you, every one can teach us great lessons. ...We cannot do without the world outside India; it was our foolishness that we thought we could, and we have paid the penalty by about a thousand years of slavery. That we did not go out to compare things with other nations, did not mark the workings that have been all around us, has been the one great cause of this degradation of the Indian mind. We have paid the penalty; let us do it no more.'[6]

Both these books appeal to me because they grapple with controversies about Vivekananda's worldview by delving deeper. They take a stand without merely 'deploying' selective quotations. For what matters today is to see our immediate challenges in the light of core values and eternal principles—that is, going beyond momentary partisan divides. In this endeavour Vivekananda remains a powerful inspiration that expands our horizon.

This book consists of three parts.

Part I: The unabridged version of articles published in *The Times of India's Sunday Review*, between May and September 1993.

Part II: An essay that I wrote, in 1993, locating my study of Vivekananda in the political context of that time.

Part III: An essay, written in 2023, reflecting on the social and political turmoil of our times in an introspective manner and sharing why Swamiji remains both a guide and a friendly fellow traveller for many of us who seek to live the full promise of his clarion call 'Brothers and Sisters'.

The reader is, of course, at liberty to read these in any order that pleases.

PART I

A Hundred Years After Swami Vivekananda's Chicago Address*

---

* Part I of the book first appeared in the form of a series of six articles in the *Sunday Review, The Times of India*—May 30, 1993; June 27,1993; July 25,1993; September 11,1993; September 19,1993.; September 26, 1993.

Preface

This series began with a gathering at Bapu Kuti, Sewagram Ashram, in January 1993. Veteran Gandhians and young admirers of M.K. Gandhi had come to commemorate J.C. Kumarappa's birth centenary and share notes on struggling for non-violent and sustainable socio-economic structures.

Over six or seven days, some of us were blessed with those rare flights of imagination and hope which occur by a seemingly magical conjunction of people, place and spirit. The base for these winged journeys was Bapu Kuti, Gandhiji's home and the dreams it houses. Yet the flight path also took us close to Swami Vivekananda's ideas about work in rural India.

This idyllic week of energising camaraderie and plans for future work, came to a jolting close as news of unprecedented communal violence in Bombay broke through the ensconcing comfort of Sewagram. When I returned to Bombay, another ten days later, the killing was still going on and fires were smouldering. The full extent of the horror began to unfold only as it became clear that otherwise responsible citizens were justifying the violence. Systematic attacks against innocent unarmed people were rationalised as a pre-emptive 'defence'. Some even argued that the Bombay killings of Muslims were a necessary retribution for killings of Hindus in the Kashmir valley.

The double trauma of finding friends and relatives turn blood-thirsty caused some people to plunge even more determinedly into relief work among victims of the violence. Others, like me, struggled just to break out of a shell-shocked state and the stupefying despair it threatened to induce.

It was then that a tiny booklet of Swami Vivekananda's thoughts on meditation suddenly appeared in the form of a rescue. He seemed to mark a pathway to being fearless, that first prerequisite for true non-violence. And the practical, moral imperative of non-violence had never seemed more real. The recent discussions at Sewagram now took on a new meaning. How could a century which began with a Vivekananda and led to a Gandhi bring us to this present? Surely such energies do not just evaporate from society? Or, am I romanticizing their lives on the basis of one-dimensional images? This meant journeying into the life and times of Swami Vivekananda. By coincidence, 1993 was the centenary year of Swami Vivekananda's Chicago address and this offered the impetus for the journalistic series. This exercise in turn led to the title-essay of this series. These articles are by way of preliminary despatches in what I hope will be an on-going journey. There is nothing new here for those who know Swami Vivekananda's life and work. But perhaps this series will interest those who know him only through the odd quotation or that famous picture where he stands proud, arms firmly folded across his chest. And I hope that it may form a small part of many friends' efforts to open and maintain dialogue in an atmosphere of polarisation, where people are finding it difficult even to laugh together.

The series was possible because of the encouragement and patience of seniors and friends, among them—Prof. M.P. Rege, Prof. Ram Bapat, Anand Bapat, Vijay Pratap, Ravi Chopra, and particularly John D'Souza, Avinash Jha and other friends at the Centre for Education and Documentation. Most of all I would like to thank the monks of the Ramakrishna Mission, in Bombay and at Belur Math, who not only made available books and facilities but stressed the importance of critical, open enquiry.

Rajni Bakshi
Bombay: March 1994

1. A Journey Begins

On a hot humid day, 100 years ago, a handsome young man dressed in bright ochre silk sailed out of Bombay on a unique mission. Naren stood on the deck of the *Peninsular* while the steamer slipped out of harbour. As he gazed at the shrinking coastline, there were tears in his eyes.

Naren's mind was crowded with memories of the people and the purpose that had put him on that ship. He thought of India and her culture, of her greatness and her suffering, of the rishis and of the Sanatana Dharma. His being was steeped in love, of this land where he had wandered alone in a determined quest.

Soon the last glimpse of Indian soil vanished over the horizon. As the blue grey waters of the Arabian sea surrounded him, the young sannyasi murmured under his breath, 'Yes, from the land of Renunciation, I go to the Land of Enjoyment.'

Who was this sannyasi and what was he going to do in the distant land of America? From tiny village huts to grandiose palaces all over India, different people knew him by different names.

Once upon a time, he had been just Narendranath Datta, son of a successful Calcutta lawyer. As a wandering monk he had sometimes been

Vividishananda—one who is trying to know many things. Elsewhere, others had known him as Sachidananda and glimpsed within him shades of its Meaning—existence, knowledge, bliss absolute. Now on the ship's log he was known as Swami Vivekananda, the name by which time and history would remember him.

To his disciples he was both revered 'guru' and a 'full of fun Swami', who enjoyed pan-supari and tobacco. He was a brooding scholar and also a merry zesty singer. Just days before the departure for America, Swami Vivekananda had described himself as a 'frolicsome, mischievous innocent.' To a guru-bhai, wishing him bon voyage, it seemed that Naren's 'heart was a huge cauldron in which the sufferings of mankind were being made into a healing balm.'

The core of this man's being, at the age of 30, was driven by the relentless zeal of a divine mission. Over a 1,000 years ago, Swami Vivekananda felt, Shankaracharya had 'caught the rhythm of the Vedas, the national cadence.' Now that same ancient music reverberated through Vivekananda's soul. But it was not enough to simply sing the beauty of the Vedanta. So, he set out on an endeavour that transcended national boundaries and sought to actively include all humanity.

This took him to a sparkling new city beside an ocean-like lake in the heart of North America. Chicago was hosting an international fair to commemorate the

400th anniversary of Columbus' accidental discovery of the 'new world'. This 'Exposition' and the World Parliament of Religions were also celebrating the dawn of the 'American Century' with its spiralling dream of limitless prosperity and ever-expanding power.

Into this world sailed that unusual monk of athletic build and luminous eyes which were shaped like lotus petals. He went uninvited, driven by the conviction that a special role awaited him there. Amid the glittering affluence of a civilisation exulting in its sense of superiority, he spoke of renunciation.

India, he said, has a special message of love to share with the world. The applause that followed his words stunned Vivekananda himself and echoed for decades. But now, across a 100 years of non-violent striving followed by brutal turmoil, history is asking us if Vivekananda's claim had any validity. In a society rapidly turning into a battlefield, conflicting sides are simultaneously drawing upon Swami Vivekananda. The bigoted and intolerant claim him as much as those who oppose such forces of darkness.

What was it about the Swami's personality, life and work that makes him today both a hero for chauvinistic Hindus and also a guiding light for people of all faiths who wish for peace on earth through a universal brotherhood of religions? The answers lie partly in the life experience of the man who could say with unabashed confidence that 'I shall inspire men everywhere, until the world shall know that it is one with God.'

As Narendranath Datta, the law student, this man had once thought that the ancient sages who saw all beings as one with God 'must have been insane.' He had read western and Indian schools of philosophy and felt that agnosticism was the only way for a thinking man. These were days of rollicking about, singing merrily on the streets of Calcutta. Brilliantly witty, Naren was the life of any party. 'His senses were keen and acute, his natural cravings and passions strong and imperious... he was no sour or cross-grained puritan,' one of his friends Brajendranath Seal later recalled. But a terrible restlessness racked Naren's being. He had practised meditation since childhood but it wasn't enough. He wanted certainty, a glimpse of the Ultimate Truth. A feeling of emptiness and sadness began to obsess him. He longed for a 'Guru or master who, by embodying perfection in the flesh, would still the commotion in his soul.'

So he sought out holy men and asked them: 'Have you seen God?' He went to Maharshi Debendranath Tagore, the leader of the Brahmo Samaj, of which Naren and his family were also members. Even the Maharshi could not give a positive answer, saying only: 'My boy, you have the Yogi's eyes.'

The answer finally came from a man who lived in a temple garden on the banks of the Ganga just outside Calcutta. 'Yes, I see Him (God) just as I see you here, only in a much more intense sense.' Sri Ramakrishna

Paramahamsa told Naren, 'God can be realised; one can see and talk to Him as I am seeing and talking to you. But who cares?'

Naren cared enough not to take anyone else's word for it. He doubted, reasoned and questioned all the way, till he felt the 'living God' within. Three decades later French philosopher Romain Rolland saw him as 'one of the first to sign a treaty of peace between the two forces eternally warring within us, the forces of reason and faith.'

These strides took Vivekananda to a cross-road. One tempting path led to the contemplative quiet of Himalayan caves. He chose the other path, which merged into the bustle of everyday human striving and suffering; for he believed that 'man is the highest symbol of God and his worship is the highest form of worship on earth.'

Thus, the multi-dimensional journey of Vivekananda's life is a tale of stupendous human will, adventure and lyrical beauty. There are clues here for understanding the ground we stand on today and perhaps signposts for helping one step across the minefield of contemporary strife.

2. Reason and Faith

He who is in you and outside you,
Who works through all hands,
Who walks on all feet,
Whose body are all ye,
Him worship, and break all other idols!

…

Ye fools! Who neglect the living God,
And his infinite reflections with which the world is full.
While ye run after imaginary shadows,
That lead alone to fights and quarrels,
Him worship, the only visible! Break all other idols!

—Swami Vivekanada

This realisation did not come easily to the merry young man who was once Narendranath Datta. But it was the essence of the journey that transformed him into Swami Vivekananda and inspired this poem.

Naren was a restless teenager. He was haunted by that eternally irksome question: 'Does God really exist?' For, if God does exist, he thought, 'then why is there no response to my passionate appeals? Why is there so much woe in his benign kingdom?'

So he floundered about, 'like a child in the wildest forest lost.'

But slowly he emerged from the thicket of doubt and uncertainty to worship 'the only God in whom I believe...my God the miserable, my God the poor of all races.' How did this happen?

The tortuous path to this realisation was lit by a frail-looking ascetic who worshipped the Goddess Kali at the garden temple of Dakshineshwar on the banks of the Ganga. This man, Sri Ramakrishna Paramahamsa, was able to say that he had indeed 'seen' God. Naren was not instantly convinced but the sincerity and confidence of Sri Ramakrishna's claim was moving.

Others already believed that Sri Ramakrishna was a Paramahamsa—one who has attained the highest spiritual state. But to Naren, at first, Ramakrishna seemed like a 'brain-sick baby, always seeing visions and the rest. I hated it.' He was not the first to say so. Ramakrishna's family had thought him insane, till a conference of pundits declared him a Divine Incarnation.

The pundits' verdict did not impress Naren either. Likewise it seemed absurd when Ramakrishna insisted that Naren was himself the incarnation of a great sage come to fulfil a divine mission. He also refused to worship the Goddess Kali. 'How I used to hate Kali and all her ways!' Naren was to say later. He was convinced that God had to be formless.

When Ramakrishna spoke of the divine revelations he experienced, Naren said: 'Who knows whether these are revelations from the (Divine) Mother or mere fancies of your brain! If I were in your position I should attribute them to imagination pure and simple.' Yet Ramakrishna's self-evident piety, his 'wonderful love' and 'marvellous purity' drew Naren. This kept him locked in an intense tussle with the man he eventually accepted as his Guru. Naren was deeply moved by Ramakrishna's insistence to 'be spiritual and realise the truth for yourself.'

So Naren continued to search and question. He ridiculed the ideas of Advaita Vedanta saying: 'I am God, you are God, these created things are God—what can be more absurd than this!' When Naren's insistence on his own view sometimes bordered on the fanatical, Ramakrishna would urge him to 'try and see the Truth from all angles and in every perspective.'

Meanwhile, the premature death of Naren's father had plunged his family into a dire financial crisis. Once accustomed to plenty, the Datta household now had barely enough to eat. Unable to find a job and provide for the family, Naren was driven to desperation.

So one day, like millions of others have done for ages, he set out to ask a favour from Goddess Kali.

As he entered the Kali temple at Dakshineswar late at night, he was 'caught in a surging wave of devotion and love.' Forgetting what he had come to ask for, he prayed instead for knowledge, devotion and uninterrupted vision of the Divine Mother. That night, he went two more times into the temple to ask for the material well-being of his family. But each time only the plea for devotion and divine benediction arose from within him.

An ineffable joy and serene peace overwhelmed Naren, and his life was never the same again. The change that came over him is to remain a mystery. Years later, as Swami Vivekananda, he said 'The thing that made me do it (accept Kali) is a secret that will die with me.'

Perhaps he felt the Super Conscious opening to him. For, later, he would say with supreme confidence that till this happened 'religion is mere talk, it is nothing but preparation.' This did not contradict or alter his commitment to reason. It only convinced him that 'all religion is going beyond reason, but reason is the only guide to get there.'

In Ramakrishna he found a living teacher and in the Buddha a timeless inspiration. 'I have more veneration for that character (Buddha) than any other—that boldness, that fearlessness and that tremendous love.'

Over 2,500 years ago the Buddha had said what Naren now felt himself: '...do not believe merely on the authority of your teachers and elders. Have deliberation and analyse, and when the result agrees with reason and conduces to the good of all, accept it and live up to it.'

Thus later, even when Swami Vivekananda preached the message of the Advaita Vedanta and extolled the Vedic civilisation, he also said: 'I take as much of the

Vedas as agrees with reason...the greatest gift God has given us.' He therefore respected people whose reason led them to be atheists, and had contempt for the blindly religious.

The person who was willing to die for God particularly worried Vivekananda. Such a person he felt, was equally capable of turning around and killing his own brother. For anyone who wanted to start a sectarian dispute, Vivekananda had this question: 'Have you seen God? Have you seen the Atman: If you have not, what right have you to preach his name—you walking in darkness trying to lead me into the same darkness...'

This certitude came from the conviction that God is not someone sitting in the clouds issuing instructions to mere mortals. God is love and within all. 'Never forget the glory of human nature,' Swami Vivekananda said. 'Be still and know that you are God.'

This realisation was earned through relentless concentration and meditation that took Naren deep inwards. Often, while meditating, he would lose all bodily sensation. He thus came, by his own labours, to share Sri Ramakrishna's conviction that the various religions are not contradictory but instead several phases of one eternal religion.

Swami Vivekananda's life journey encompassed many of these phases and extended far beyond. He was simultaneously a devout worshiper of Kali, the unseen life force of the universe, and an untiring admirer of the Buddha. The greatness of Buddha, above all human beings in history, was sealed by his dying words: 'Let there be no false bondage, no dependence on me... The Buddha is not a person, he is a realisation. Work out your own salvation.'

But then personal salvation alone cannot be the goal of one who truly finds an ideal in the Buddha. Seeking the salvation of others is even more important. Swami Vivekananda had a firm conviction that salvation did not depend on the grace of God—because 'freedom always is.' Even the pursuit of spiritual ecstasy is not enough. 'To serve Narayana, you must serve the Daridra Narayanas—the starving millions of India.'

This was also the ambitious task that Sri Ramakrishna had set for his disciples. In his last years, while he battled painfully with cancer, Sri Ramakrishna identified a select group of disciples, many of them westernised middle-class Bengali boys, to carry on this work. Naren was the spiritual inheritor of the 'Master', as they called Sri Ramakrishna, and the natural leader of the band of sannyasi disciples.

These disciples aimed to demonstrate the special ideal of unity among religions by having the spirituality of Hindus, the mercifulness of Buddhists, the activity of Christians and the brotherhood of Mohammedans.

Over the next decade and a half, following Sri Ramakrishna's death in 1886, Naren's life was a struggle to simultaneously realise this universal ideal and also to fulfil a mission within the Hindu fold. These were not automatically complimentary tasks. Swami Vivekananda struggled to make them so, just as he had forged his own path across the apparent contradictions between faith and reason.

One kind of restlessness had taken Naren to Sri Ramakrishna's doorstep. Now anchored to mysterious strengths he gave way to a new restlessness, a wandering urge that dominated the rest of his short life.

3. Indian Odyssey

By stretching the imagination one could still picture the peaceful Ayodhya of a hundred years ago. Perhaps it was there, meditating on the banks of the river Sarayu, that Swami Vivekananda was inspired to see Sita as the ideal of India. For, he said, 'Sita knows no bitterness...she never returned injury.'

In reality, however, the itinerant sannyasi found that India often did not live up to this ideal. But meandering across the country, puzzling over its history, he realised that India's life as a civilisation depended on her people—on their striving to truly be Sita's children. And he insisted that every Indian has it in them to try.

This confidence was wrought in the course of a legendary journey across time and space. Its guides were eternal ideals like Sita and human embodiments like Buddha and Sri Ramakrishna Paramahamsa. The path was illuminated by the Buddha's conviction that 'when a man hurts you, you turn back to hurt him, that would not cure the first injury: it would only create in the world more wickedness.'

But do we focus on this while commemorating Swami Vivekananda's 'Bharat Yatra' a century later? Or are we content to celebrate his life as a declaration of Indian greatness and not look at the motivating force which propelled it?

Why in this land of high spiritual achievements, is there so much injustice, indignity and poverty? This question haunted Naren long before he embarked on the Indian odyssey and emerged from it to become famous as Swami Vivekananda. The answers came to him gradually from a close study of the homeland and self-awareness of his own responses.

Once, weary after a long trek, Naren was cheered to see a man by the roadside contentedly smoking a pipe. With all the ease and camaraderie of a fellow smoker he went up to the stranger and asked for a puff from the chillum. The villager looked up at the imposing figure in ochre clothes and shrank back shaking his head. 'It would defile you, sir,' he said, 'I am a bhangi (sweeper).'

Naren too instinctively pulled back. Continuing down the road he felt uneasy and disturbed. As a sannyasi he aspired to be above notions of caste and prestige. 'Yet I fell back into caste ideas when the man told me that he was a sweeper... That was due to ages of habit.'

Suddenly, he turned around, went back to the villager and said 'Brother do light me a chillum.' The mystified man agreed to share his chillum only after much persuasion. Centuries of conditioning had convinced him that he was an 'outcaste', duty-bound to protect the 'purity' of the upper castes by staying out of their way.

On hearing about this incident, the sannyasi's friends

teased him saying that it only showed his addiction to smoking. The young aspirant to renunciation probably laughed along. But he knew it wasn't that simple. People like that wayside stranger made Naren feel, within himself, the tenacious grip of old social customs that divide people. His diligent struggle for 'sameness of vision' could not be just a quest for spiritual ecstasy. It was also a tussle to liberate himself from false duality in practical life. This effort, in which he did not always succeed, went on till the end of his 39 years. As he once wrote to a friend: 'If ever I get true renunciation, I shall let you know.'

But all of his life was not a sombre struggle. From Calcutta to Porbundar and Almora to Kanyakumari, the learning was accompanied by a sheer enjoyment of adventure and affection for strangers who became friends.

Naren reached Agra in the monsoon of 1888 and was enthralled and overpowered by the Taj Mahal. For days, he just stared at it from every possible angle because 'every square inch of this wondrous edifice is worth a whole day's patient observation and it requires at least six months to make a real study of it.'

In Lucknow, he was 'lost in admiration of the splendours bequeathed by the Nawabs of Oudh, and of the city's gardens and mosques.' The imperial grandeur of Delhi left him physically and spiritually elated. According to his disciple biographers, the Swami 'found in Delhi the symbol of the immortal glory of the Indian people, with its grand, composite culture.'

But the collective memory of the same people was also filled with the pain inflicted by rulers, who lived on the blood of their subjects. Swami Vivekananda sensed this and was preoccupied with problems which persisted 'even if the kings be of as god-like a nature as that of Yudhishtra, Ramachandra, Dharmashoka or Akbar, under whose benign rule the people enjoyed safety and prosperity.' For such paternal care provided 'no occasion for understanding the principles of self-government.' This perpetual dependency on kings for everything gradually drained people of their inherent energy and strength.

Were Puranic tales about near perfect kingdoms mere fantasy then? Swami Vivekananda decided that it was in most cases impossible to decipher historical facts out of myth and legend. But studying the ancient scriptures convinced him that there had been an age of brilliant Vedic seers and valorous noble kings to match. Yet even then, the same society had also been busy inventing its own hurdles. 'Liberty is the first condition of growth,' the Swami wrote to Alasinga Perumal, one of his closest disciples. 'Your ancestors gave every liberty to the soul, and religion grew. They put the body under every bondage, and society did not grow.'

Thus Hinduism accumulated the loftiest teachings on the dignity of humanity but 'no religion on earth treads upon the necks of the poor and low in such a fashion as Hinduism.' Once, in a moment of blazing anger, Vivekananda wrote: 'The whole world looks down with contempt upon the 300 millions of earthworms crawling upon the fair soil of India and trying to oppress each other.'

But his mission was to improve, not worsen, the already low Indian self-confidence. Swami Vivekananda lived at a time when many kinds of bitterness were rife. A certain class of Indians had begun to see themselves as 'losers' in the race of nations and some were eager to shift the blame for all their ills to foreign invaders, beginning with the Muslims over a thousand years ago. For Swami Vivekananda this approach amounted to self-evasion. Even he saw India as an enslaved nation, but primarily because of its own failings and missed opportunities. 'The Lord once more came to you as Buddha and taught you how to feel, how to sympathise with the poor, the miserable, the sinner but you heard Him not,' he wrote. 'Your priests invented the horrible story that the Lord was here for deluding demons with false doctrines!... So you are bond slaves to any nation that thinks it worthwhile to rule over you.'

But even Buddhism had internally decayed and weakened before it could be driven away by the old priestly class. There emerged then an alliance of mutual self-interest between the priests and the royal class— both now sans their former moral values. This union, being 'inherently steeped in vice,' led to the 'sucking of the blood of the masses, taking revenge on the enemy, spoliation of others' property...' Such rulers were thus 'cheap and easy prey to the Mohammedan invaders from the West.'

In spite of his sage-like equanimity, Vivekananda had a deep contempt for all those who used force to spread their religion. He vehemently denounced the violence of Islam and Christianity in certain phases of their history. But he also knew that coercion alone did not cause conversions. Islam won adherents with its message of equality. Christianity with its message of love.

As he roamed across India, the Swami had lengthy discussions with several Muslim maulvis on both Islamic and Hindu philosophy. He concluded that the differences between the Hindu and Muslim worlds were more apparent than real. The national ideal, for Swami Vivekananda, was drawn from the teachings of the ancient sages and thus essentially Hindu. But he saw no inherent conflict between this and the distinct stream of Indian Islam. 'Shah Jehan would have turned in his grave to hear himself called a 'foreigner',' the Swami once told a disciple who had erred in so describing the Mogul emperor.

By the time he reached that last bit of Indian rock off the coast at Kanyakumari, Swamiji had acquired a lucid clarity about his mission. Without abandoning his internal critique of Hinduism, Vivekananda decided that there had been enough fault-finding in the 19th century. The time had come for reconstructing and building strength.

For Swami Vivekananda this meant that 'the epithet "mild Hindu", instead of being a word of reproach, ought really to point to our glory...how much development of qualities of love and compassion have to be acquired before one can get rid of the brutish force of one's nature, which actuates the ruining and slaughter of one's brother-men for self-aggrandisement.'

The regeneration of Hinduism required Hindus to have renewed confidence in these ideals and themselves. Non-injury can be a living faith only for those whose confidence and sense of self-worth is deeply rooted. What then, does the violation of these ideals in Ayodhya itself tell us about ourselves today?

Following Swami Vivekananda more closely, as he leaps into the sea at Kanyakumari and later heads West, may help to understand what we are today and offer renewed hope in being able to rise to finer levels of realisation and being.

4. A Plan for India

'At Cape Comorin sitting in Mother Kumari's temple, sitting on the last bit of Indian rock—I hit upon a plan: We are so many sannyasis wandering about, and teaching the people metaphysics—it is all madness. Did not our Gurudeva used to say, "An empty stomach is no good for religion?"'

—Swami Vivekananda

The athletic, young sannyasi sat perfectly still on an off-shore rock at Kanyakumari. Steeped in deep meditation he seemed to have reached a realm beyond time, space and the tingling salt spray of crashing ocean waves. This image of Swami Vivekananda, at the rock that now bears his name, is one of modern India's most enduring legends.

The glare of adulation has tended to obscure the tumultuous human struggles of that legendary persona. And these struggles are the clue to why even a century later Swami Vivekananda, and his plans for India, inspire people across the ideological spectrum. Let us journey back a hundred years to see what bothered Vivekananda and served as an impetus for his sense of mission.

Wandering as a pilgrim, from the Himalayas to India's southernmost tip, Swami Vivekananda saw: 'A country where a million or two sadhus and a hundred million or so of Brahmins suck the blood out of these poor people, without even the least effort for their amelioration—is that a country or a hell? Is that a religion or a devil's dance?'

So he resolved to undo these injustices and revitalise India by saving religion from those who made it a 'devil's dance'. But this ambitious aspiration had to contend with global forces that were beyond any single man's influence.

Looming large over the threshold of the 20th century, Swami Vivekananda saw 'modern western science dazzling the eyes with the brilliancy of myriad suns and driving in the chariot of hard and fast facts.' By the late 19th century western materialism and colonialism had come to dominate the world. By comparison the Indian civilisational endeavour seemed to have atrophied. The colonial encounter had shaken the self-confidence of Indian society as never before.

In addition the efforts of Christian missionaries to convert 'heathens' had triggered anxieties within sections of Hindu society. Swami Vivekananda's self-defined task was to simultaneously eliminate the evils in Hindu practice and also reaffirm the value of the tradition. Thus he felt compelled to assert that 'Hinduism is not a mistake.' Herein lay one of his most intense struggles.

As a disciple of Sri Ramakrishna Paramahamsa and a diligent spiritual aspirant, Swami Vivekananda sought the essentials of Hinduism in pure spirituality. As an activist entangled in the throes of history, he sought the common bases of Hinduism in order to unify its diverse strains. The insights of Vedanta provided these common bases and gave the Swami a means of synthesizing his inner quest and his worldly mission.

The essence of this mission was to demystify spiritual truths—bringing them out of the monasteries and the hold of priest craft. Since the objective was to retrieve the highest ideals of the existing religion, Swami Vivekananda placed the greatest onus for this revitalisation on orthodox Hindus. He held them responsible for the fact that essential principles had languished over the centuries and decayed internally. What were these essentials?

Religion, Vivekananda said over and over again, is realisation. Rituals, colours, 'mantras' and idols may help, but these were not the essentials of a spiritual life. He believed, 'If your heart has not opened, if you have not realised God, it is all in vain.' And purification of the heart requires 'worship of the Virat—of all those around us.'

Religion and spirituality, so defined, was in Vivekananda's view the common ground for the amalgam of cultures in India. And restoring health to these essentials of religion was, for the Swami, a necessary prerequisite for the rejuvenation of India. All these convictions added up not to one but many 'plans'. There had to be a 'man-making' education, both spiritual and scientific, that would give strength to the people. Additionally, the making of a great future India required 'organisation, accumulation of power, coordination of wills.'

But when he arose from his meditation on the rock at Kanyakumari, the high tide of ideas was also accompanied by a dogged restlessness. He was not sure exactly how all this would add up to both, filling empty stomachs and saving religion. Besides, all plans demanded selfless dedicated workers and funds. The wandering mendicant had a few followers but no funds. So he decided to go to America to spread the message of Indian spirituality and to earn money.

Behind the glitter of western affluence Swami Vivekananda sensed another kind of decay and crisis. So he saw himself as a missionary who must seek a mutually enriching synthesis of eastern and western thought. But would preaching 'the incomparable glory of the Vedas and the Vedanta' necessarily be compatible with his goal of fostering universal religion? For Vivekananda, the two were one and the same. His notion of 'conquering' the world with spirituality was based on the faith that 'love must conquer hatred, hatred cannot conquer itself.'

Thus, bursting with a 'tremendous power and energy' Vivekananda set forth on the solitary voyage to America and the Parliament of Religions where history waited to test his faith.

5. Children of Immortal Bliss

'As the different streams having their sources in different places all mingle their water in the sea, so O Lord, the different paths which men take through different tendencies, various though they appear, crooked or straight, all lead to Thee.'

The Catholic cardinal sat at centre-stage in crimson robes. On both sides of him were other devout followers of 'different paths', gathered for the unprecedented Parliament of Religions. There were Buddhists in flowing white robes and the Greek Orthodox Christians in sombre black, leaning on ivory sticks.

At one end of this platform of diverse faiths in their distinct colours sat Swami Vivekananda in gorgeous red robes and a bright yellow turban. The characteristically confident exterior veiled his anxiety. He had neither a prepared speech nor much experience in public speaking.

'My heart was fluttering and my tongue nearly dried up,' he was to write later. 'I was so nervous and could not venture to speak in the morning.'

Just when it seemed doubtful whether the Hindu monk would speak at all, Swami Vivekananda arose to share the above prayer with that unique gathering. Bowing to Devi Saraswati, he began—'Sisters and Brothers of America...' Suddenly to his utter amazement, hundreds of people in the audience were on their feet, applauding. 'Here was a soul greeting thousands of other souls in sweet and loving terms—"Sisters and Brothers",' one eye-witness later recalled. '...Or was it the Divine power behind him that seized the audience by a whirlpool of spiritual ecstasy?'

This event took place on 11th September 1893 at the Art Institute of Chicago. Today, a hundred years later, while the legend of Swami Vivekananda's success at the Parliament of Religions lives on, few know exactly what he said. It is generally believed that he did the Hindus proud. But was Swami Vivekananda's action a claim of Hindu greatness? Or, was it a call for mutually respectful give and take between different religions—an expression of the hopeful potential of all humanity? The time had come, Vivekananda said in his opening speech, to root out the 'horrible demons' of sectarianism, bigotry and fanaticism which had destroyed entire civilisations. The bell that tolled at the start of the Parliament, he hoped, would be 'the death-knell of all fanaticism, of all persecutions with the sword or with the pen, and of all uncharitable feelings between persons wending their way to the same goal.'

This sentiment had already been expressed by others at the Parliament. What sealed Swami Vivekananda's place of prominence in history was the enfranchising declaration that all human beings were inherently 'Children of Immortal Bliss.'

'Allow me to call you brethren, by that sweet name—heirs of immortal bliss—yea, the Hindu refuses to call you sinners!' said Vivekananda in his main speech called 'Paper on Hinduism'. '...Come up, O lions, and shake off the delusion that you are sheep; you are souls immortal, spirits free, blest and eternal; ye are not matter; ye are not bodies; matter is your servant, not you the servant of matter.'

God—'the pure and formless one, the Almighty and the All merciful,' he said, was to be worshipped not out of fear but through love. Far superior to loving God for hope of reward, in this or the next world, was 'to love God for love's sake.'

Worship in this sense needs no specific or exclusive formula. Therefore, in Vivekananda's interpretation, 'the Hindu religion does not consist in struggles and attempts to believe a certain doctrine or dogma, but in realising—not in believing but in being and becoming.'

'The Hindu may have failed to carry out all his plans,' he went on to add. Yet, the concepts of spirituality that evolved in India, Swami Vivekananda argued, had a special contribution to make, in building a future universal religion and a true brotherhood of all humanity.

The Parliament of Religions signalled both this

striving for a 'universal religion' and the difficulties in making it a reality. Swami Vivekananda himself was attempting to simultaneously affirm universal brotherhood and yet to take a firm stand, as a Hindu, against Western cultural imperialism.

The Parliament of Religions was part of a larger Exposition which was a self-conscious display by the United States of America as an emerging super-power. Underlying the liberalism implicit in a 'parliament' of religions, was an unquestioned confidence in the primacy and superiority of Christianity.

Just as Swami Vivekananda's decision to go to America had been stiffly opposed by Hindu orthodoxy, the organisers of the Parliament were also under considerable pressure. The Archbishop of Canterbury had refused to send a representative because, he said, 'Christianity is the one religion.' Attending the Parliament would mean conceding 'the equality of other included members and the purity of their position and claims.'

Such views hovered in the background of the Parliament and later dogged Swami Vivekananda's efforts in the West. Some American critics ridiculed Vivekananda as 'a man who came out of a land that had been dead and buried for 5,000 years and talked of renunciation.'

So while Swami Vivekananda was the star of the Parliament he did not quite conquer the West. Yet in certain circles, he did make a deep and lasting impact. This was partly due to the transparent authenticity of his convictions. Even while he denounced the methods of Christian missionaries, his deep reverence for Christ's message was self-evident. Thus, the Boston Evening Transcript wrote in April 1894: 'There is infinite humiliation in this spectacle of a pagan priest reading lessons of conduct and of life to the men who have assumed the spiritual supervision of Greenland's icy mountains and India's central strand but the sense of humiliation is the sine qua non of most reforms in this world.'

This was the context in which Swami Vivekananda's success at Chicago became a matter of pride for Indians. This was particularly so among Hindus, some of whom hailed the Swami as the first Hindu 'missionary'. The Swami's success boosted the emerging struggle against the smugness of the colonial culture. But it did so with an appeal for enhancing human civilisation as a whole on terms of mutual respect, eschewing aggression and conflict. This is what makes Swami Vivekananda a 'live' historical personality a century later.

But his legacy is now ironically caught in bitter controversy. One set of claimants to the legacy are preoccupied with asserting Hindu 'pride' in vengeful and aggressive terms vis-a-vis other religions. And then there are those inheritors who strive to realise the ideal of universal brotherhood of all religions.

To understand the nature of this striving we need to look closely at what Swami Vivekananda meant by 'Universal Religion' and how it can be realised. This may also help us to see why these closing words of the Chicago address could mark the dividing line between genuine religiosity and bigoted fanaticism: '...upon the banner of every religion will soon be written, in spite of resistance: "Help and not Fight", "Assimilation and not Destruction", "Harmony and Peace and not Dissension."'

6. Quest for Universal Religion

'They are very sincere people, these fanatics, but they are quite as irresponsible as other lunatics in the world. This disease of fanaticism is one of the most dangerous diseases. All the wickedness of human nature is roused by it. Anger is stirred up, nerves are strung high, and human beings become like tigers.'

—Swami Vivekananda

The cyclonic sannyasi knew he would not live to be 40. So the remaining nine years, following his instant fame at the Parliament of Religions, were spent in a whirlwind of activity. Travelling widely across America and Europe he taught, learnt and pursued his spiritual quest with intense vigour.

These encounters with diverse cultures confirmed Swami Vivekananda's view that religion had given humanity both 'the intensest love' and 'the most diabolical hatred'. So he set out to explore if a universal religion, a brotherhood of different faiths, was at all possible. Let us begin, Vivekananda suggested, by recognising that there cannot be, and ought not to be, a universal philosophy, mythology and symbols: '...for I know that this world must go on working, wheel within wheel this intricate mass of machinery, most complex, most wonderful. What can we do then?' asked the Swami. 'We can make it run smoothly, we can lessen the friction...By recognising the natural necessity of variation.'

This requires us to 'learn that truth may be expressed in a hundred thousand ways, and that each of these ways is true as far as it goes.' The vision of God may vary in every case, 'yet he is one...this is the only recognition of universality that we can get.'

Countless saints and seers have reiterated this elementary truth for centuries. Yet, most efforts for a brotherhood of religions failed for want of a practical plan which would show people the point of union with all other faiths without destroying the individuality of any religion.

Over the years Swami Vivekananda worked out the rudiments of such a plan and anchored it with this maxim: 'Do not destroy.' He urged people to build instead of pulling anything down. 'Help if you can; if you cannot, fold your hands and stand by and see things go on. Do not injure, if you cannot render help.'

Secondly, the Swami suggested, 'take a man where he stands and from there give him a lift. If it be true that God is the centre of all religions, and that each of us is moving towards him along one of these radii, then it is certain that all of us must reach that centre. And at the centre, where all the radii meet, all our differences will cease.' And, he insisted, we can all teach ourselves to get there. 'None can make a spiritual man out of you...your growth must come from inside.'

Such growth is, according to Swami Vivekananda, the only way to check the latent 'tiger' in us. This is vital for human civilisation because the fanatic uses not merely swords but contempt, social hatred and social ostracism against all those who do not agree with him. On the other hand, the rational man is glad that others do not think exactly as he does. Since thinking beings must differ, 'variation is the sign of life, and it must be there.'

A celebration of this variation would be universal religion. The ideal may seem elusive but Vivekananda believed it to be inherent to human striving. 'If the priests and other people that have taken upon themselves the task of preaching different religions, simply cease preaching for a few moments, we shall see it is there.'

These were the elements that Swami Vivekananda challenged within his own faith. And the central mission of the Swami's life was within the Hindu fold. As he often said, the Hindu might believe that unity in variety was the plan of Nature. But, in practice, bitter sectarian disputes and layers of superstition had obscured these universalist and humane principles. Vivekananda struggled to retrieve them.

It was in this context that he called Buddhism 'the fulfilment of Hinduism.' He urged that the Brahmin intellect must join 'with the heart, the noble soul, the wonderful humanising power of the Great Master (Buddha).'

Swami Vivekananda's mission to galvanise Hindus and make Hindu society dynamic was a multi-dimensional endeavour. But at its core was the exhortation for this 'fulfilment' to become a part of living practice. Then it might be possible for Hinduism to actually embody the ideal of universal religion as Vivekananda had defined it in the Chicago address:

> 'It will be a religion which will have no place for persecution or intolerance in its polity, which will recognise the divinity in every man and woman, and whose whole scope, whose whole force, will be created in aiding humanity to realise its own true divine nature.'

Since the Swami was a man of action, and not just ideas, his energies were severely over-taxed in this last decade of his life.

The magnitude of his spiritual, social and organisational mission drove him at a pace which made fatigue inevitable. But the Swami's disciples believe that exhaustion alone could not overcome that superhuman will. They recall his guru Sri Ramakrishna Paramahamsa's prediction that Naren would leave his body the day he realised his true self. Perhaps it was that realisation which allowed the Swami to slip away one evening in 1902. He had often visualised his own departure from the body, murmuring, 'Hara, Hara (The free, the free).'

Yet, the words which resound through his life journey, and perhaps make a fitting epithet are these: 'Love never fails, my son; today or tomorrow or ages after, truth will conquer... Believe in the omnipotent power of love.'

PART II

The Dispute Over Swami Vivekananda's Legacy: A Warning and an Opportunity (1993)*

* An earlier draft of this essay was presented at a seminar at the Institute for Development Studies, Jaipur, in August 1993.

The present dispute over the legacy of Swami Vivekananda brings to mind the pre-battle skirmishes of the Mahabharata. As their armies prepared to take position at Kurukshetra, the warring cousins vied bitterly for the allegiance of their many common relatives. Once the polarisation was complete the stage was set for a war from which there could be no victors, only heart-broken survivors.

The quarrel over Swami Vivekananda should be a warning signal for a society with the epic consciousness of the Mahabharata. This futile dispute cautions us about degenerating into a fratricidal conflict in which all common ground and natural affinities are thoughtlessly disregarded. It also offers us an opportunity to pause and reconsider the nature of escalating tensions in society and seek new ways of transcending them. But this is possible only if we suspend the tug-of-war method. The search for ways out of the present darkness cannot be marred by a discourse that is implicitly premised on notions of perennial conflict. Besides, the duelling mode of 'debate' only legitimises that approach to human interaction and history which found expression in the destruction of the Babri Masjid in Ayodhya.

Let us then, by an act of faith, mark the parameters of this discourse with a shared commitment to preventing Indian society from becoming an all-consuming battlefield. Having done that, we may also attempt to shun the methods and language of 'use'. Then the entry into Swami Vivekananda's world-view can be fittingly marked with these words of Sister Nivedita:

"The "purifying of the heart" connoted the burning out of selfishness. Worship is the very antithesis of use.'[1]

Swami Vivekananda is significant a century after he lived and worked, precisely because of this struggle for 'Chittashudhi' which runs through his life and work. The value and meaning of these struggles tends to be minimized when Swami Vivekananda is attributed oracle-like powers or viewed through the haze of adulation as a certified national hero and patriot. He did, in part, fill many of these roles with a larger than life presence. But the best way to travel with him seems to be as companion—simultaneously questioning and trusting, irreverent and affectionate.

I would like here to share a small part of my attempt to journey thus with Swami Vivekananda. Narendranath Datta started out in life as a doubting agnostic and grew into a devout servant of God. By the time he came before the world as Swami Vivekananda, the young sannyasi was both a 'jnani' and a 'bhakta'. Such a transformation is not uncommon. But in Narendranath's case it was marked by a rigorous commitment to synthesising reason and faith. All religion, he decided, 'is going beyond reason, but reason is the only guide to get there.'[2]

Even while he studied the Vedas with reverence Swami Vivekananda accepted only that part which agreed with reason. Thus even though he disagreed with much of Buddhist doctrine, the Buddha was the one person Swami Vivekananda revered above all others in human history: 'Buddha never bowed down to anything—neither Veda, nor caste, nor priest, nor custom. He fearlessly reasoned so far as reason could take him. Such a fearless search for truth and such love for every living thing the world has never seen.'[3]

Narendranath's eventual 'surrender' to Goddess Kali was preceded by an intense and bitter struggle. The essentially mystical experience did not contradict the Swami's commitment to reason. Eventually he explained it thus: 'Religion is neither talk, nor theory, nor intellectual consent. It is realisation in the heart of hearts; it is touching God; it is feeling, realising that I am a spirit in relation with the Universal Spirit and all Its great manifestations.'

Swami Vivekananda's inner being remained ever faithful to this quest. But as a spiritual aspirant inspired by Buddha and guided by Sri Ramakrishna Paramahamsa, personal salvation could not be the central goal of his life. Thus his mission was to demystify spirituality, free it from the shackles of priest-craft and make it accessible to people of all classes, castes and creeds. But Vivekananda was also an activist entangled in the worldly throes of history. It is this dimension of his mission that preponderates over our present.

By the time Swami Vivekananda's wanderings

across India culminated at Kanyakurnari, his sense of 'mission' was as multifaceted as his personality. While his moorings were in eternal principles, the worldly concerns of Swami Vivekananda were shaped by his times. Therefore, retrieving pure spirituality from the vast diversity of Indian philosophical traditions was not enough.

As he travelled to America and saw nations on the move, Swami Vivekananda felt the full force of changes and challenges posed by the modern era. He located himself between the religious tradition and those strains of an emerging Hindu middle-class that had begun to function entirely in the Western frame of knowledge. To the orthodox pundits he appealed that the contents of Hinduism be submitted to the test: 'For this reason we must come out of the limited grooves of the past and take a look at the world as it moves onwards to progress at the present day. And if we find that there are hidebound—customs which are impeding the growth of our social life or disturbing our philosophical outlook, it is time for us to advance a step by eschewing them.'[4]

Likewise he could fall with 'thunder-bolt vehemence' upon those who spoke in a belittling manner of the 'the meaningless teachings' of the Vedic seers: 'How dare you criticise your venerable forefathers in such a fashion! A little learning has muddled your brain. Have you tested the science of the Rishis? Have you even as much as read the Vedas? There is the challenge thrown up by the Rishis! If you dare oppose them, take it up: put their teachings to the test.'[5]

Poised confidently at the cross-roads of divergent trends in Indian society, Swami Vivekananda set out to question the bigotry and prejudices of orthodoxy, as well as the crisis of self-confidence among the classes closely inter-acting with the West. He traced India's degeneration to its people's loss of faith in themselves. Over the years Swami Vivekananda elaborated a historical analysis of this decay which need not be detailed here. It will suffice to mention that he traced the roots of decay to ancient, pre-Buddhist times. Internally the Swami identified the need for a liberality which would allow both religion and society to breathe freely and grow.

Yet underlying the sharp critique were anxieties about Hinduism's ability to stand up in modern times, not only as a cohesive body of thought and practice but also as a distinct and confident member of the family of world religions. Thus he sought the common bases of Hinduism. Sister Nivedita, perhaps the most prolific and outstanding of Vivekananda's disciples, believed that his whole life was a search for the common bases of Hinduism.

This search led Swami Vivekananda to identify two essential commonalities between the plethora of Hindu sects—the Vedas and belief in God as: '...the creating, the preserving power of the whole universe, and unto whom it periodically returns to come out at other periods and manifest this wonderful phenomenon, called the universe.'[6] The lecture (in Lahore), at which Swami Vivekananda elaborated this theme, also illustrated his tension between the universal and particular. At one point he said: 'Ay, we often mistake mere prattle for religious truth, mere intellectual peroration for great spiritual realisation, and then comes sectarianism, then comes fight. If we once understand that this realisation is the only religion, we shall look into our own hearts and find how far we are towards realising the truths of religion.'[7]

Swami Vivekananda applied this universal principle to the task of galvanising Hindus into a cohesive group, which for him was a move against sectarianism: 'Then and then alone, all sectarian quarrels will cease, and we shall be in a position to understand, to bring to our hearts, to embrace, to intensely love the very word Hindu and everyone who bears that name. Mark me, then and then alone you are a Hindu when every man who bears the name, from any country, speaking our language, becomes at once the nearest and the dearest to you.'[8] Was this not an exclusivist definition of what it meant to be a Hindu? Within Swami Vivekananda's own frame of thought it was not so. He was convinced that a 'true' Hindu would have to be above all sectarianism. For the Hindu ideal, Vivekananda believed, was not 'tolerance' but acceptance: 'Toleration means that I think that you are wrong and I am just allowing you to live. Is it not blasphemy to think that you and I are allowing others to live.'[9]

Therefore the Swami was firmly unforgiving about the intolerance and violence of all religions—whether it was Islam and Christianity's 'conversions by the sword' or Brahmanical Hinduism's brutality to shudras. Just as he denounced the exploitative ways of Hindu priest-craft yet sought to reaffirm the 'ideal' of a Brahmin, Vivekananda denounced the violence of Islam and yet identified with the philosophic men within Islam who protested against the cruelties.

Swami Vivekananda's life reflects the interface of Hinduism and Indian Islam at the close of the 19th century. Even a cursory account of his life, from childhood to sage and abbot of Belur Math, would illustrate the closely inter-linked social and cultural life of Hindus and Muslims. The Swami could enthral his disciples by rendering the coronation song of Akbar 'in the very tone and rhythm of Thanasena [Tansen].'[10] But his life also reflected how, even after a thousand years of co-existence with it, Islam was still seen as an 'outsider'. Vivekananda would speak of how 'The sword had flashed, and "Victory unto Allah" had rent the skies of India; but these floods subsided leaving the national ideals unchanged.'[11]

Even while he resented the historical role of Islam, at certain periods of history, as an activist committed to revitalising not only Hinduism but the whole of Indian society, he saw the necessity for a more active give and take between Hinduism and Islam. He realised that it was easy to talk glibly about the Vedantic ideal of oneness of all beings. Hindu society had done this for centuries while also practising many forms of inequality and virtual apartheid. Thus Swami Vivekananda suggested that the Vedantic ideal of oneness needs a social body imbued with the spirit of equality and fraternity. And, in this respect, Islam had made greater strides. He wrote to Sarfaraz Hussain—described in *The Life of Swami Vivekananda* as 'an Advaita Vedantist at heart'—who became a disciple of the Swami and took the name Mohammedananda: 'I believe it (Advaita Vedanta) is the religion of the future enlightened humanity...I am firmly persuaded that without the help of practical Islam, theories of Vedantism, however fine and wonderful they maybe, are entirely valueless to the vast mass of mankind...For our own motherland a junction of the two great systems, Hinduism and Islam—Vedanta brain and Islam body—is the only hope...'[12]

Yet some germ of anger with the 'invader' nagged Swami Vivekananda till late in his brief life. The destruction of temples bothered him and he struggled with this emotion. Then, writes Sister Nivedita: 'He came back, in Kashmir, from one of the great experiences of his life, saying with the simplicity of a child, 'There must be no more of this anger.' Mother (Devi) said: 'What even if the unbeliever should enter My temples, and defile My images, what is that to you? DO YOU PROTECT ME? OR DO I PROTECT YOU?' (Emphasis in original.)

'His personal ideal was that Sannyasin of the Mutiny, who was stabbed by an English soldier, and broke the silence of fifteen years to say to his murderer,—And thou also art He.'[13]

That Sannyasin also embodied what was for Swami Vivekananda the Indian ideal—Sita, who knew no bitterness and never returned injury.[14]

Of course Sita does not become India's ideal because Swami Vivekananda believed so. Yet there must be more than poetic significance in the Swami's intense and rigorous life finding its centre in this ideal. On this note let us shift to the present day situation and travel to Mathura-Vrindavan.

In January this year (1993), an assortment of left-wing activists and some members of the Rashtriya Swayamsevak Sangh (RSS) met at Vrindavan to attempt a dialogue. The meeting, called 'Samvad Prayas', had been planned several months in advance and originally included a much wider range of participants. Many people had withdrawn following the destruction of the Babri Masjid, and the unrepentant stand of the RSS and its affiliates, because there now seemed to be no scope for dialogue. Others who condemned the destruction of the masjid and yet attended the meeting, went with a great deal of trepidation and came away with a deep sadness.

Perhaps the visit to the temple known as Krishna Janmasthan will illustrate the nature of the problem. Just beside this relatively smaller temple stands a grand, five or six stories high, temple built perhaps in the last half century. Directly behind this towering edifice is a mosque of older vintage but nearly matching proportions. One of the younger RSS activists asked, with apparently genuine bafflement, why the sight did not bother me. On the contrary, I attempted to explain, it is for me a reassuring and enriching sight. But just as I could not understand the outraged sentiments of that young man, he could not fathom how I could view those adjacent houses of worship as a symbol of beauty and highly evolved cultural strengths.

Like the unsuccessfully attempted 'Samvad Prayas' this exchange also demonstrated how, unresolved questions about, the Hindu-Muslim equation in post-Partition India are not at the core of what ails us today. The threat of fratricidal conflict alluded to earlier does not pertain essentially to Muslim-Hindu tensions, but to the self-destructive polarisation that seems more and more to pervade public discourse.

It is in this context that Swami Vivekananda has become the focus of a bitter dispute between the proponents of 'Hindutva' on the one side and liberal, secular, democratic view point on the other. By a strange coincidence the destruction of the Babri Masjid has taken place in the centenary year of Swami Vivekananda's famous Chicago address. But those responsible for the action, a body of organisations affiliated to the RSS, also claim Swami Vivekananda as their hero. They seem indifferent to the tragic irony of how their vandalism in Ayodhya on 6th December has undermined the claim for peace and tolerance which Vivekananda made on behalf of Hindus at the Chicago Parliament of Religions.

In a fragmentary way the RSS does conform to some of Swami Vivekananda's ideas about galvanising Hindus through dynamic organisation and service. But cultivation and legitimisation of communal hatred, which is implicit in the RSS world-view, was clearly not a part of the Swami's agenda. His dream for rejuvenating Hinduism was at its core an internal challenge of retrieving strengths—a return to intelligent spirituality cutting across the plethora of superstition and thoughtless repetition of ritual.

The manner in which Swami Vivekananda linked the revitalisation of Hinduism with that of India as a nation is a contentious issue.

How this indirectly contributed to the perception of the non-Hindu as, a sometimes offensive, 'other' remains a question. However, the present war of quotations involving Swami Vivekananda's works does nothing to help answer such questions or build an understanding of our past and present. Instead it further worsens the overload of tension in public life. This is partly because this quarrel is dominated by those who are using Swami Vivekananda for some narrow partisan interest. A genuine debate may offer ways of appreciating how the universal appeal of Swami Vivekananda offers possibilities of exploring common ground among different people who may have conflicting viewpoints but not ruthlessly competing agendas.

The urgency of this endeavour has been brought home not merely by the demolition of the mosque but by the active and tacit consent given to the demolition by a wide cross-section of people in different classes. In one sense Swami Vivekananda's worst fears have come true. Such rampant and brutal sectarianism implies an erosion of spiritual values. And it is these values, Swami Vivekananda believed, which are the life-blood of India. Their decline would mean the death of the civilisation.

However, the purpose of invoking Swami Vivekananda in the contemporary debate is not to serve as a voice of doom. Nor is there much point in going to him as an oracle. The importance of his life rests in how he grappled with various contradictory pulls. These were pressures generated by the exigencies of India's struggle not only with colonialism but the multiple challenges of modernity. In this context Swami Vivekananda struggled simultaneously to retrieve the humanist strains of the tradition and socially and philosophically strengthen Hinduism for its encounter with the modern era. My reading of the Swami's works and those of his contemporaries is far too inadequate for a thorough understanding of this endeavour to reshape Hinduism and locate it in the 20th Century.

I am merely suggesting that a genuine debate on Swami Vivekananda's life and world-view may enhance our understanding of forces that shaped our present and will help us grope our way out of the present darkness. This firstly demands a commitment to preventing a decline towards all-consuming conflict. This means exploring the spaces between the shrill and vicious propaganda of 'Hindutva' and the still largely silent disquiet among believers of the diverse layers of Hindu society.

This will also mean that those of us who have never accepted the notion of 'injured Hindu pride' as an issue of contemporary relevance will have to concede the objective reality of this perception and attempt to understand why this remains a vulnerable sore. So far most anti-communal efforts have focused on the vested interests who have manipulated this perception of injured pride for narrow and short-sighted political gain. It is doubtful whether those who brazenly justify historical vengeance as a valid form of social mobilisation, can be engaged in a meaningful dialogue. But there is a vast body of people who may willy nilly support the rhetoric of 'Hindutva' ideology without agreeing with the full agenda of its votaries. Perhaps Swami Vivekananda's works offer a common ground for dialogue between such people and those who altogether oppose the preoccupation with 'symbols of defeat'.

The exercise could begin by addressing just one question. At the time of Swami Vivekananda's unexpected and overwhelming success at the Parliament of Religions, Indians celebrated the restoration of their pride and honour. In the context of the traumatic on-going encounter with Western colonialism, in the 19th century, this was understandable. There followed, in the next half century, a burst of creative energies and activities which seemed to imbue the society with a fresh vitality and self-confidence. That process, though far from complete, is an on-going endeavour. Why then are some Indians now feeling a need assert their pride by settling historical scores that add no creative, constructive worth to national life? How can the terms of discourse be altered to shift the focus inwards and seek reasons for needing an enemy, some 'other', who can be blamed for assorted failures of a civil society and state policy?

PART III

A Personal Reflection: Wherefore Now? (2023)

Take a man where he stands, and see how he may go forward from there.

Swami Vivekananda often said this in the context of a person's spiritual journey, or lack thereof. As I look back on my three decades of *satsang* and the seeking of truth in the universe of Swamiji's thought, and striving, this appeal by him to approach people with hope and empathy, is the essence of how his presence has inspired and energised me.

I have understood this appeal to apply in all those situations when we feel that someone, some 'other', is taking a wrong stand—one that we deem to be 'backward' or unhelpful both for that individual's own well-being and of those around them.

Have I tried to live by this advice? In a limited and modest manner, yes—even when I judged my own effort or its outcomes to be inadequate, at times quite a failure. I have persevered in trying to understand where a person 'stands', why they feel or think as they do and if there might be some fundamental values upon which we can agree.

The tumultuous conflicts that have torn through India in the 30 years since the demolition of the Babri Masjid in 1992, have provided rather an excess of opportunity to practise this approach. Naturally, the same times have also provided ample opportunities for inner and outward growth. The distance travelled over that period is, first of all, evident in how I now view the title I chose for the essay written in 1993. 'Dispute Over Swami Vivekananda's Legacy: A Warning and an Opportunity' now seems overly prosaic and lacking in imagination. More importantly, in 2023, there is an objective basis for saying that this title is past its expiry date—that the 'warning' was long ago dismissed, ignored, rejected. From newspaper columns and speeches on political platforms, to conversations within families and the frenetic frontiers of social media—it appears as though India's polity and samaj are now bitterly polarised.

There is also a frequently heard claim that this polarisation is unlikely to be reversed anytime soon and 'damage control' is now the only mode of action open to those who worry about communal tensions and want peace and justice. My purpose here is to reject this defeatist approach and instead explore possibilities on another track.

Even if the polarisation is as pervasive as it seems— we are still at liberty to defiantly work for moral renewal that nurtures various forms of fraternity within India's samaj. Indeed, if one is committed to seeking how anyone may go forward from where they are now—this search within samaj is imperative.

When I first sought refuge in the collected works of Swami Vivekananda all I could see were two opposing sides in a tug of war—like armies on a battlefield vying for dominance. On one side were those who celebrated the demolition of the Babri Masjid as an act of valour that restored Hindu pride. On the other side were those who condemned the same action as an act of desecration driven by vengeance and hatred.

In 2023, those who celebrated the demolition of the Babri Masjid appear to be victorious. In the purely material dimension, this appears to be true. In January 2024 a grand Ram Temple, built on the site of the demolished mosque, will be inaugurated with a nationwide celebration. Those who see the new Ram temple in Ayodhya as a symbol of rectifying past wrongs have a louder, more pervasive voice. Those who challenge this view or refuse to join in the celebration are treated with disdain or condemned for either not respecting 'Hindu sentiments' or being out-right 'anti-Hindu'. For each 'side' to condemn the other is easy, but futile. Swami Vivekananda's philosophy is vital to this moment because he compels us to consider if we can reach out to the 'other' in a spirit of restoration and reconciliation. This inspiration then can open the way to exploring if there are indeed two 'sides'? Is there really a binary divide? The perception of a binary divide, though materially compelling, is a bit like sinking into a black hole. Thirty years ago, I experienced the pull of this black hole, when I felt caught within a metaphorical tug of war—of being on a 'side' that was locked into a perpetual conflict.

But what if, in reality, we are in the midst of a

manthan—a churning? I am not invoking here the imagery of the mythic 'Samudra Manthan' between the Devas and Asuras. Although that myth is imbued with many subtle complexities, it is commonly perceived as a tug of war in which the Devas won. The churning I refer to is an inward process we all experience—that swirl of competing emotions and diverse dimensions of our own 'self', which is not about winning or losing but knowing yourself more deeply and clearly.

This churning is a process of discovering more about yourself by understanding the other.

A tug of war in society is often about one identity group or interest group trying to be victorious over some 'other'. In comparison, churning within a samaj is about recognising and processing competing impulses in ways that enable all to evolve and grow. But why then is Vivekananda important to this moment of churning in Indian society? Why do forays into Vivekananda's world, his thoughts and aspirations, have such a compelling allure more than a century after he left the mortal coil?

Before exploring these questions in detail, it is vital to reiterate some points made in the essay written three decades ago. It is a grievous error to seek out Vivekananda as though he were an oracle. It is still more unfortunate to 'use' Vivekananda as a source material for propaganda that the two sides can throw at each other. That is tug-of-war behaviour. Vivekananda continues to inspire because his life itself was a kind of manthan—because he was constantly processing the turmoil of impulses and counter-responses. This 'processing' remains precious for us today because the endeavour had a firm spiritual, philosophical and moral anchor.

If we see ourselves as swirling and tossing, like in a churning, then it is the processes of Swamiji's life rather than his pronouncements that become all important. It is in being able to relate to Vivekananda's inner struggles that we enrich our own lives. Primarily because in our own different ways we are facing similar struggles—not necessarily in some public or political contest but in arguments with friends and family.

In 2023, the apparent divides take many forms—Hindu Rashtra vs Secular India, Hindutva vs Hinduism, Hindu vs Muslim, Bharat vs India, fundamentalists vs moderates, and so on. I will neither attempt to fully describe nor explain the complex terrain on which these contests are playing out. Nor will I aim to comprehensively examine these divides through the lens of Vivekananda.

Instead, my purpose here is limited to sharing how and why my understanding of Vivekananda's richly colourful and adventurous life has both challenged and inspired me over the last 30 years and why it still remains a source of strength, lending confidence to remain a part of the churning.

I will aim to do this by sharing a few stories which, in an introspective spirit, explore how Swamiji does have answers for one of the key issues of our times—the challenges posed by the feelings of hurt Hindu pride and the possibilities for a revitalization of Hindu samaj. To put it simply—how can Swamiji help us to manage or overcome fear and grow love?

This means we have to look closely at the energies and *bhava*/feelings that make up the *taana-baana,* warp and weft of samaj—that non-material ground on which we live our lives and process our fears, joys and longings.

It is only fair to disclose at the outset that for me, the core of Swamiji's inspiration remains the same. If I were to write that series of articles today, it would still conclude with these words:

> 'Love never fails, my son; today or tomorrow or ages after, truth will conquer...Believe in the omnipotent power of love.'

But it is not enough to celebrate this insight, this appeal, as an abstract truth. We must be able to explore how this truth can be an energy that guides our actions amid the violence and hatred. This is not a small or light-weight challenge. Violence and hatred grab more attention, they are in-your-face. Whereas the energy of truth and love seems more amorphous and subtle. It helps if we doggedly look for nuances and refuse to take a monochromatic view of reality.

My purpose here is to:

One, share what I have learnt by looking for nuances.

Two, consequently understand with empathy, the crisis of self-esteem that lies at the heart of hurt Hindu pride.

Three, most important of all, explore how Vivekananda's life and thought are part of a sequence of rich experiences over the last century that can serve as inspiration for a revitalized Hindu culture.

Vivekananda's inner journey and mission in the world offer not ready-made answers but important insights that can strengthen and enrich us as we grapple with the challenges of our times.

Beyond a monochromatic view of reality

Sometime in 1992, Dharamvir Bharati, veteran Hindi journalist and celebrated literary figure, visited Ayodhya to talk to those living in the vicinity of the 16th century Babri Masjid. The structure was believed to have been built at the behest of Babur, the first Mughal king—though this remained a matter of contestation between historians. Similarly, there is no agreement on just when it was first claimed that this mosque was built on the birthplace of Sri Ram, Prince of Ayodhya, son of King Dasharath and the chief protagonist of the epic Ramayana. By the early 1990s, even advocates of the Ramjanmabhoomi (Birthplace of Ram) campaign were saying that no historical evidence is required—it is sufficient that people believe that the Babri Masjid stands on the birthplace of Ram.

After having followed the bitter dispute over the Babri Masjid from afar for many years, Bharati felt it was time to go to Ayodhya in person. By then, an unsuccessful attempt had already been made by votaries of the Ramjanmabhoomi campaign to demolish the 400 years old structure. Tens of thousands of volunteers, from across India, had assembled for this purpose. That attempt had failed and the Babri Masjid remained solidly in place. As Bharati stood in front of this imposing structure, he started a conversation with an elderly woman who happened to be passing by.

This woman, a Hindu, had come to Ayodhya as a pilgrim from a nearby village. Bharati pointed to the Babri Masjid and asked the woman if she was in favour of a Ram temple being built on that spot. With a simplicity devoid of any rancour the woman said: 'It would feel good to have a Ram temple at the birth place of Sri Ram.'

Then Bharati pointed to the minarets of other mosques in Ayodhya. He asked her: 'What about those mosques? What about the mosque in your village?'

The woman was puzzled by this question. She could not understand what Bharati was asking. He then explicitly asked whether she felt those other mosques in Ayodhya or the mosque in her village should also be demolished.

'Certainly not!' came the emphatic reply. For her there was no connection between the wish to see a Ram temple at what she believed to be the birthplace of Ram and the existence of mosques where her Muslim neighbours could worship.

Bharati's story reminded me of why Vivekananda regarded Sita as the essence of India—because she never returned injury. That woman whom Bharati spoke with did not want a Ram temple in place of the Babri Masjid out of resentment or as vengeance. Therefore, she could want the new Ram temple while respecting and honouring other mosques in Ayodhya and her own village.

We, the votaries of a humane liberal secularism, inadvertently helped to sharpen the conflict by not paying enough detailed attention to the sentiment expressed and represented by that old woman. It is also painfully true that the hate filled propaganda of the campaign to tear down the Babri Masjid left little or no room for such voices to be heard. 'Musalman ke do hi sthaan, Kabristan ya Pakistan' (There are only two places for Muslims, graveyard or Pakistan) was one of the common slogans shouted during the many processions and public gatherings of the Ramjanmabhoomi movement.

Some votaries of the Ramjanmabhoomi campaign did share that old woman's nuanced approach. But the sweeping effect of that campaign was to obliterate this nuanced distinction between wanting a Ram temple and holding no grudge against Muslims. Even more importantly, that campaign also revealed the fault lines between very different approaches to being Hindu.

Ramchandra Guha's account of what happened when, in 1992, several veteran Gandhians went to Ayodhya to oppose the call for demolishing the mosque, is worth recalling here:

> 'Shortly before the Babri Masjid was destroyed, a group of Gandhians visited Ayodhya. They were led by a woman named Sushila Nayar, an 80-year-old physician who had worked closely with Mohandas Gandhi. A prayer meeting conducted by Nayar ended in the singing of Raghupati Raghava Raja Ram, a favourite hymn of Gandhi. When they came to the line "Ishwar Allah Téré Naam" (God is named both Ishwar and Allah), the meeting was disrupted by shouts and slogans. A section of the crowd surged towards the stage. Nayar came down to explain to the protesters that the singers had come "on behalf" of Gandhi. "Aur hum Godsé ki taraf sé," the disruptionists are said to have replied: we have come on behalf of [Gandhi's assassin] Nathuram Godse, and like him we think you Gandhians are too soft on the Muslims.'[1]

At the time when this incident took place, such a brazen claim in favour of Gandhi's assassin was rare and this incident evoked wide spread condemnation. Three decades later it has become common-place for Gandhi to be denigrated and his assassin to be valorised. This does not mean that all advocates of Hindutva support the glorification of Godse. But most of them do see the phenomenon as a side-effect of what they crave—the consolidation of a strong Hindu identity. Underlying this aspiration is the lingering crisis of self-esteem, or hurt Hindu pride. Vivekananda had an intimate understanding of this condition.

Crisis of Self-Esteem

Narendranath Datta was born on 12th January 1863, just five and a half years after the first war of Independence in 1857. The 1860s were the decade in which, having crushed the Indian 'rebellion' and taken over from the East India Company, the British crown was consolidating its power in its most important colony. Vivekananda grew up in a reasonably affluent family in Calcutta, then the capital of the British Raj. The idea that the British could rule over Indians because they are intellectually and organisationally, perhaps even racially, superior was common-place. It was a default assumption.

Vivekananda's guru Sri Ramakrishna Paramahamsa was, of course, free of this delusion. The guru's training and blessings were certainly a key to the shaping of Vivekananda but the additional advantage was Vivekananda's insatiable curiosity and a hunger for knowledge. This also meant that he was unwilling to simply be 'given' answers and instead needed to arrive at them through his own investigation and reasoning. Therefore, by 1888, when he left Calcutta and the company of his brotherhood of monks to became a Parivrâjaka—a wandering monk, Vivekananda was confident of the spiritual and historical foundations upon which he stood.

The next four years of wandering across India brought him face to face not just with the many miseries suffered by millions but also the crisis of self-confidence among Indians in general and Hindus in particular. *The Collected Works of Swami Vivekananda* show that Swamiji was prone to flashes of anger over the many injustices he witnessed. This anger was, more often than not, inwardly focused as he forged a self-critical assessment of the Indian samaj. While on one hand, he was anguished by the negative impacts of those who came from outside India and exploited its people, he was far more hurt and disturbed by the brutalities and injustices perpetrated by Indians upon each other. Looking back in time, Vivekananda concluded that the Buddha was a vital evolutionary leap in this sub-continent's spiritual evolution because he taught love and compassion. Thus, Swamiji often lamented that it was rejecting the Buddha that turned Indians into slaves.*

---

* See Page 42 for more details

However, while Vivekananda had a searing critique of the flaws in our samaj, he did not limit his perspective to just 'problem solving'. Instead, he dedicated his life to framing a positive vision of renewal and re-creation.

There appear to have been two aspects of the crisis of self-confidence that Vivekananda witnessed. The predominant aspect was related to the pervasive phenomenon of Indians in the modern elite and emerging middle class, who dismissed or rejected the Indic civilization as being inferior and claimed that this was why the British were ruling over the sub-continent. The other aspect was the unease, even anger, of Hindus in relation to Muslims and Christians.

Therefore, the cultivation of the militant spirit among Hindus was important for Vivekananda, but it had a vital pre-condition—the cultivation of moral rigour and self-discipline. For these are the requisite steps towards self-realisation. And he was certain that there is no hope for the liberation of the Indian people as a whole, unless there is a determined effort for self-realisation at the individual level. Vivekananda's premise is that only human beings who are at least striving for self-realisation and moral advancement, can renew and strengthen Indian society. It is not a coincidence that later in the 20th century, M. K. Gandhi built a powerful dimension of India's freedom struggle on this same premise.

Vivekananda's brief public life, from 1893 to 1902,

happened at the threshold of a paradoxical historical moment. The development of young Narendranath Datta into Swami Vivekananda was possible only because he found living proof of the highest spiritual attainments in his guru Sri Ramakrishna Parmahamsa, who left this world in 1886. Later, at the cusp of the 19th and 20th century, India was further blessed with the presence of several great souls—though their presence and influence on the world stage unfolded in different ways over the half century following Vivekananda's physical departure from this world. Aurobindo, Anandmayi Maa, J. Krishnamurti, Narayana Guru, Ramana Maharshi, Sarada Devi, Yogananda—are just some of the spiritual seekers whose life and work revitalised Indic spiritual traditions and, in some cases, regenerated and 'updated' associated social practises in the 20th century.

The paradox is that the presence of these great souls was not sufficient to counter the toxicity generated by the British colonial government's decision in 1905 to partition Bengal—between the eastern side which had a majority population of Muslims and the western side which was predominantly Hindu. This action evoked a passionate resistance from the secularist-nationalist movement *but* it also boosted the parallel rise of Hindu nationalism and Muslim nationalism. Eventually, by the 1940s, the idea that there were 'two nations' on this sub-continent, one Hindu and the other Muslim, gathered credence and led to the birth of a partitioned, free India.

Memories of the holocaust of communal violence which accompanied Partition remain a sore, which is often scratched to stoke animosity between Hindus and Muslims even 76 years later. Ironically, this has continued even after the birth of Bangladesh, the formation of which should have debunked the claims of the two-nation theory based on religion. The birth of Bangladesh, after a brutally violent struggle for independence, proved that language identity and regional cultural affinity was more important than religion.

The paradox is that, in the first half of the 20th century, numerous political and spiritual leaders showed by example that to be truly religious is to be compassionate and that it is neither automatic nor inevitable that religion puts one in competition or conflict with some 'other'. At the same time, various organisations, both Hindu and Muslim, fostered exactly the opposite belief, exhorting millions of people in South Asia to feel bitter hatred towards each other.

Hindu nationalism came to be based on the claim that Hindus had suffered a thousand years of foreign rule—first, with Muslim raiders from the West, later the rise of Muslim sultanates and dynasties across India, and finally followed by British colonialism. While Vivekananda was aware of the brutal events in the past, he was equally, if not more, drawn to the many signs of syncretic culture which he found in his travels across the sub-continent.

Instead of hating and resenting present day Muslims because people of their faith had in the past raided or ruled over Hindus, Vivekananda sought to identify that which made Hindus weak and how this could be rectified by reforms within. He was disturbed by the destruction of Hindu temples in the past but refused to make this the motivational force for being a Hindu now.*

Those who today feel that enmity between Hindus and Muslims is unalterable may argue that Vivekananda cannot offer a guiding light on this issue because he did not live to see the 20th century conflicts between these communities. But they should also then either ignore, deny or reject Vivekananda's anchor in Advaita—the awareness that all life on earth, indeed consciousness in the cosmos, is part of one indivisible whole. This firm faith is what empowered Vivekananda to stand firmly against all internecine disputes between communities, while at the same time opposing injustices in ways that would heal and foster harmony.

In Vivekananda's time it was common for Indic traditions in general and Advaita philosophy in particular to be dismissed as being 'other-worldly'. This

---

* See Page 70 for more details

was denounced as a failing and identified as the defining characteristic of Hinduism. The argument extended further to point out that this was what made India weak and/or backward. Vivekananda stood against this ignorance with all his might. Even more importantly he aimed to do this through love and compassion. That he left behind written records of his own internal struggles with moments of anger and hurt is what makes him an inspiration across the ages and also makes him a figure that ordinary people can relate with.

For instance, Vivekananda's confidence that Sita is the essence of India because she does not return injury is not to be taken lightly.* This confidence has been repeatedly reaffirmed by people living and working long after Vivekananda. It is a stream of energy which continues to thrive and merits a brief overview.

Seeking At-one-ment

In December 1992, perhaps in the same week that the Babri Masjid was demolished, a seminal narrative was published by the philosopher, Ramchandra Gandhi. It was titled *Sita's Kitchen: A Testimony of Faith and Inquiry*. Ramu Gandhi, as he was fondly known, was a spiritual seeker, teacher and a grandson of both Mahatma Gandhi and C. Rajagopalachari. *Sita's*

---

* See Pages 38 and 71 for more details

Kitchen opened with Ramu declaring himself to be an Advaitin and a disciple of Ramana Maharshi (1879-1950), a mystic saint who lived in Tamil Nadu.

Like Dharamvir Bharati, Ramu had been drawn to the disputed site in Ayodhya while the mosque still stood. In the compound of the Babri Masjid, he was struck by the sight of a small shrine marked 'Janmasthan sita ki rasoi', which consisted of nothing more than a chakla-belan—a chapati-making rolling board and a rolling pin. For Ramu this shrine signified the connection between the birthplace of Rama, and Sita as Sakti—Mother-earth. In those simple instruments of everyday domesticity, Ramu saw symbols of nurturing love and regeneration.

The presence of the Sita ki Rasoi at Ayodhya thus was a reminder that despite the turmoil and upheavals over centuries—across caste and religious denominations—the people of this sub-continent have worshiped nature itself as an omnipresent divinity. Locating himself deep inside the tradition of Advaita Vedanta, Ramu went beyond the dominant dispute of that time—namely whether or not there was a temple at that site before the Babri Masjid. He rather suggested that it was far more important that this site had once been an ancient sacred grove.

Curiously enough Ramu did this without knowing that 'Sita ki Rasoi' is a motif and a shrine across the tribal communities of central India. In the early 1990s,

I would often visit the tribal villages of the Narmada valley, where tens of thousands of people were struggling to save their homes and fields from being drowned in the submergence zone of the Sardar Sarovar Dam. In many of those threatened tribal villages there were Sita ki Rasoi shrines and the space around them was sacred just as the river Narmada has been sacred to countless generations of tribals and non-tribals. 'Sita ki Rasoi' is also a tattoo pattern which is frequently applied among tribals of central India. It represents plenitude and abundance.

The deep roots of Adavaita and its rejection of dualism as seen in Sita ki Rasoi is as much a phenomenon in aboriginal spirituality as also a more formal Hindu, Buddhist and Jain traditions. Therefore, Ramu proposed that the best way to honour the spirit of Sita ki Rasoi was to turn Ayodhya into the venue for a sub-continental congregation of atonement not merely between Hindus and Muslims but more importantly between humans and the rest of nature. By 'atonement' Ramu did not mean redress, expiation or penance but 'onement'—unity of human beings with each other and with nature as divinity.

In a lyrical exploration of what is the 'self' and how the self might relate to 'others', Ramu crafted a moral framework which could transform the Ramjanmabhoomi issue from a conflict to an opportunity for social and spiritual renewal.

Though its writing style was not technically philosophical, this book sold few copies and remained almost unknown to the general public despite being published by a major publisher. *Sita's Kitchen* was remarkable in the timing of its publication but Ramu was not alone in reaching deep within Hindu traditions to seek answers that would align spiritual truths with contemporary aspirations to build a good society.

Prabhash Joshi, the celebrated editor of the major Hindi daily newspaper *Jansatta*, was another passionate advocate of a Hindu culture that is inherently plural and humane. As an intellectual of the Gandhian Socialist tradition, Joshi repeatedly made the case for how the fundamentals of Hindu philosophy can bolster the ideals of the Preamble of India's Constitution. Joshi's writings in *Jansatta* and other Hindi newspapers reached millions of readers across North India with well-reasoned arguments, based on his own experience of living traditions, to show that neither tradition nor modernity sanction the hate-filled campaign of the Ramjanmabhoomi movement.

In 2003, in a book titled *Hindu Hone ka Dharam* (The Dharma of Being Hindu), Joshi began by highlighting that the roots of Hindu nationalism are in the late 19th century and the Ramjanmabhoomi campaign is an outcome of that history. His exploration of what it means to be Hindu was anchored in the core values of social, economic and political justice. His purpose was 'bandhutva'—fraternity—which in action means a commitment to dignity for all. Therefore, the demolition in Ayodhya was a trauma for Joshi. He called it an 'ahindu'—an anti-Hindu action. What is at stake, he wrote on 7th December 1992, are the traditions that have thrived for thousands of years without which neither India nor Hindus can be true to themselves.

Likewise, Ashis Nandy, the political psychologist, argued against nationalism itself. Nandy argued that once a society endorses nationalism—in the form of one country, one religion, one language—religion actually becomes irrelevant. Nandy pointed out that Vinayak Damodar Savarkar, the Hindu nationalist ideologue who developed the term 'Hindutva', was not himself religious. Neither was Mohammad Ali Jinnah who led the formation of the Islamic Republic of Pakistan. This also explains why votaries of Hindutva tend to appear impervious to the criticism that their ideology is inconsistent with the essential values of Hinduism.

Nandy also highlighted a vital distinction between nationalism and patriotism. The former is an ideology, the latter a sense of belonging, the feeling of a certain area or region being home. A nation and nationalism, Nandy said, calls for a homogenised population. In the case of nationalism love of the country tends to go along with specified enemies and friends, allies and detractors whereas patriotism thrives on overlapping and multiple identities. In one particular conversation Nandy made this point by quoting what Khan Wali Khan, Abdul Ghaffar Khan's son, said in a Pakistani court: "'My Lord, I am a Pakistani for 45 years, Muslim for 1400 years and a Pathan for 5000 years." So he knew that he has multiple selves and some selves will often have priority over other selves.'[2]

Since the early 1990s social and political groups working for communal harmony have sought to celebrate the multiple and over-lapping identities that come naturally to people of the Indian sub-continent. They have also specifically drawn upon various shades of humanism in Hindu traditions. For example, in the early 1990s, advocates of the Ramjanmabhoomi campaign coined the following slogan, which became commonly visible as a sticker in public places:

'Garv se kaho hum Hindu hain' (Say with pride we are Hindus)

The communal harmony groups responded with:

'Prem se kaho hum insaan hain' (Say with love we are humans)

Thus, it was only natural that a communal harmony network that sprang up in Mumbai, following the carnage in Gujarat 2002, named itself 'Insaaniyat'. The reasoning behind this emphasis on humanism was theoretically sound. We were seeking the roots of that fellow-feeling which under-grids life itself. As a participant in many such forums, I say with confidence that we believed elementary humanism to be the anchor for 'We the People' of the Preamble of India's Constitution.

At the same time, we were not blind to the reality that a large number of people experience their caste and religious identity in a much more visceral manner than 'citizenship'. The emphasis on insaaniyat was a way of urging people to focus on the core values that sustain life and thus resist efforts to divide them on the basis of religious or caste identity.

This understanding remains unchanged for me and yet my way of responding has evolved over the last three decades. Now when someone says, aggressively or otherwise, 'garv se kaho hum Hindu hain', my response is to ask if they would consider changing that to *'prem se kaho hum Hindu hain'*. I do this because it allows me to place the emphasis on 'prem' or love and hopefully avoids an argument over why I am invoking 'Insaan' rather than 'Hindu'.

The invocation of 'garv' or pride, in that slogan, may well be experienced by many as an affirmation of the highest ideals that they equate with being Hindu. For them it may well be similar to someone saying 'I am proud to support democracy' or 'I am proud to stand for human rights'. Yet in practise the 'garv se kaho' slogan was too often loaded with resentment about being belittled or somehow slighted as a Hindu.

Those making a clinical assessment of hurt Hindu pride might argue that these feelings of hurt and resentment have to be processed through social and political events. This need for processing certainly cannot be cut short by a counter-call for love. What is difficult, or even impossible, to know is this: does said process have to play out through external events or is it necessarily an inward process that can work both at the individual and collective level.

By emphasising 'prem se kaho hum Hindu hain' my peers and I are building upon many centuries of lived experience which shows that prem/love can be an antidote to hurt pride. This knowledge shines through in the poetry of the bhakti saints across India. It is not a coincidence that in the last 30 years young people have re-discovered the bhakti poets. Kabir festivals and Kabir yatras have become a regular feature in many parts of urban India. Much of this is purely cultural activity on the surface but the love and compassion being celebrated are an increasingly important political statement.

Such energies are commonly dismissed as being infinitesimal compared to those groups and individuals who, both randomly and in an organised manner, are violating fundamental rights. The starkest evidence of this are acts of violence targeting Muslims, planned or spontaneous.

In such a situation, how is one to draw a living and practical inspiration from Vivekananda's ideal?

'My ideal indeed can be put into a few words and that is: to preach unto mankind their divinity, and how to make it manifest in every moment of life.'—Swami Vivekananda (laminated card from the Ramakrishna Mission)

For most human beings this is a tall order. But is this really too lofty an ideal, one to which life rarely rises?

Vivekananda lived this ideal firstly by speaking the truth as he saw it. Thus, he was outspoken about how much this ideal is violated in practise. 'No religion on earth preaches the dignity of humanity in such a lofty strain as Hinduism, and no religion on earth treads upon the necks of the poor and the low in such a fashion as Hinduism.'[3]

On the ground, Swamiji manifested his ideal through an ethics of sewa/service. 'Since God manifests in the form of human beings, one actually serves God by serving others,' Swami Medhananda writes in his book *Swami Vivekananda's Vedāntic Cosmopolitanism*. He quotes Vivekananda talking to the fellow disciples of Sri Ramakrishna:

'What Thakur [Ramakrishna] said today in his ecstatic mood is clear: One can bring Vedanta from the forest to the home and practice it in daily life. Let people continue with whatever they are doing; there's no harm in this. People must first fully believe and be convinced that God has manifested Himself before them as the world and its creatures. ...If people consider everyone to be God, how can they consider themselves to be superior to others and harbour attachment, hatred, arrogance—or even compassion (daya)—towards them? Their minds will become pure as they serve all beings as God (sivajnane jiver seva), and soon they will experience themselves as parts of the blissful God. They will realize that their true nature is pure, illumined, and free.'[4]

Wherefore now

One:

It may be good to start with a resolve—to not get caught within the maze of immediate and narrow political contentions which present the human condition in its darkest forms. For then there is a risk of losing touch with the basic truth that life is sustained by love, compassion and cooperation. If this seems counter-intuitive when we are caught in the throes of a conflict, let us consider the significance of Vivekananda's frequent references to 'the worship of the terrible'.

When I first began reading Vivekananda, this exhortation about the worship of the terrible disturbed and puzzled me. So, I sought the help of Swami Ranganathananda, who was then a senior monk of the Ramakrishna Mission. He later became its President.

What does this 'worship of the terrible' mean? I asked him. I also told him how terrified I was of the 'terrible', which I saw as rearing its head in the form of communal violence.

On the day I met him, Swami Ranganathananda was unwell. Even though he had to lie down, he was still meeting seekers and answering their queries. Sensing the intensity of my distress he raised himself partially, resting on one elbow. 'The worship of the terrible,' he said, 'means that we don't have a goody-goody or partial understanding of the divine. Worship of the terrible means that we seek to know divinity by accepting all dimensions of reality.'

I understood this to mean that to merely wish away wickedness is to make one's self weak. To acknowledge its existence, to bow to the wicked as Tulsidas does in the opening pages of Ramcharitmanas, can enable one to grapple with it from a position of strength. Then one is better able and more steadfast in the task of vanquishing the evil deeds, instead of the evil doers.

This was the core insight that guided Mahatma Gandhi's politics—that it is the wrong doing, the injustice, that must be corrected and this can and must be done without demonising or obliterating the person who is committing that wrong. Vivekananda is crucial to the practise of this because he helped us to see that the aggressive and destructive tendency is present within all of us. He called it the latent 'tiger' within each one of us. Some of us are able to keep this 'tiger' in check and some are not. Vivekananda saw the fanatic, of any kind, as someone who is ruled by this tiger within. And who is the fanatic? It is someone, says Swamiji, who uses not merely swords but contempt, social hatred and social ostracism against all those who do not agree with them. The rational man is glad that others do not think exactly as he does because thinking beings must differ, since variation is the sign of life.

This is why Vivekananda was confident that the bell that tolled at the start of the Parliament of World Religions in Chicago signifies 'the death-knell of all fanaticism, of all persecutions with the sword or with the pen, and of all uncharitable feelings between persons wending their way to the same goal.'

The confidence that this is possible and worth striving for, is all important. But what does it mean to put this confidence into practice?

For instance, those who cheered the demolition of the Babri Masjid in 1992 and now celebrate the newly constructed Ram temple in Ayodhya may have 'uncharitable feelings' towards those who regard the demolition and all that has followed as a shame. The reverse may be equally true. If both sides remain frozen in a position of mutual contempt then neither side has even a chance of overcoming 'contempt, social hatred and social ostracism'. On the surface it does indeed look as though this mutual contempt has intensified over the last 30 years. So, what then is the way forward?

It might help if we recognise that some degree of moral dissonance seems to be an inescapable facet of the human condition, though it keeps manifesting in new forms and contexts. Practising 'cancel culture' on those whom we feel are guilty of acute moral dissonance does little more than increase the sum total of 'contempt, social hatred and social ostracism'. Historically, this is true as much for so-called 'right wing' movements as it is for 'left-wing' movements. This happens when a 'cause' is deemed to be all important and then contempt and violence are supposed to be treated as 'understandable', as a necessary tool. Treating a goal as being so lofty that any 'means' can be justified is a recurring and nagging problem of diverse social and political struggles.

In this context, perhaps the most vital inspiration we can draw from Swamiji, is to keep reminding ourselves that 'the death-knell of all fanaticism' cannot be a point of arrival. It is necessarily an arduous and on-going process. If we treat it as a destination then we are bound to blame and resent those who seem to be obstacles on the way. Instead, if we focus on refining the processes that enable us to actually *live* this aspiration, or even live *for* it, then limitless creative possibilities open up, however painful and difficult the journey might be. In a nutshell, hating the hater neither helps anyone nor improves the social and ethical conditions in which we live.

Two:

This does not make the path any easier because most of us do experience 'uncharitable feelings' or have ignoble thoughts. This happens even while we are committed to the fundamental values of compassion and love. In everyday life it can be excruciatingly difficult to deal with the violations of those fundamentals—namely unconditionally equal right to life and dignity for all. Here we come face-to-face with the practical difficulties in striving to take a person where they stand and explore how they may go forward from there. It is easy enough to know that hating the hater does not improve either the external situation or our own sense of well-being. But how do we grapple with the swirling tumult of emotions?

Processing that tumult in a self-critical and introspective manner helps. For instance, I have no personal experience of 'injured Hindu pride'. This does not mean that I should trivialise the feelings of those who do have this experience. In the public discourse, it has commonly been argued that the upsurge of 'injured Hindu pride' is a consequence of systematic and effective propaganda. This is largely true and yet it is not a holistic depiction of our reality.

The raw feelings of hurt pride, however vaguely present, existed before they were mobilised and weaponised by a distinctive ideological project— Hindutva. Assiduous effort has been made to keep scratching this hurt pride. How then can this reality be addressed at a human level in a humane manner? Vivekananda is relevant to this process but not in a comforting manner.

For instance, I am deeply inspired by Swamiji seeing Sita as the ideal of India. He said, 'Sita knows no bitterness...she never returned injury.' In practical terms, this means that I must firstly process my own feelings of discomfort, let alone animosity, towards those who advocate returning of injury and settling of scores in varied forms. The challenge lies in reaching out to them without anger or counter-bitterness about their bitterness! This ambitious undertaking is eminently worthwhile even if it is bound to involve quite a bit of stumbling and floundering.

This effort is worth making because it is compatible with the 'physics' of the human condition. Vivekananda puts it as follows, attributing this insight to the Buddha: 'When a man hurts you and you turn back to hurt him, that would not cure the first injury: it would only create in the world more wickedness.'

Gandhi expressed this incontestable truth famously in a still more graphic manner—'an eye for an eye would make the whole world blind'.

Three:

Even if one accepts this nonviolent frame, the crisis of self-esteem being experienced by many Hindus remains. It still needs to be addressed and in this regard Vivekananda's life experience, not just his analysis or readings of texts, are vital.

Firstly, he openly documented his own feelings of

anger and bitterness about the past—not just as a Hindu but as someone who felt a deep sense of belonging to the plural heritage of the Indian sub-continent. Secondly, he intricately explained how his learnings at the feet of Sri Ramakrishna, along with the experiences of his travels, enabled him to process these feelings and free himself. The story, narrated by Sister Nivedita, about Swamiji's experience of anger at seeing destroyed Hindu temples and later his encounter with Goddess Kali in Kashmir is instructive because it records this very transition from feelings of anger to freedom.*

This is why Vivekananda sought to galvanise Hindus on the basis of love. For love sets you free whereas anger and hate, as afflictive emotions, hold you captive. His notion of 'conquering' the world with spirituality was based on the faith that 'love must conquer hatred, hatred cannot conquer itself.'

It was on the basis of this inner freedom that Vivekananda crafted an internal critique of Hinduism and on that basis made a case for renewal and revitalisation. For Swamiji, the term 'mild Hindu' was not a reproach, as many saw it to be, both then and now. Instead, his emphasis was on acknowledging that it took centuries to develop the qualities of love and compassion which enabled people to be rid of the brutish elements of human nature.

---

* See Page 70 for more details

In the next four and a half decades after Vivekananda passed away, M.K. Gandhi dedicated himself to living by this truth. He wrote in his autobiography: 'To see the universal and all-pervading spirit of Truth face to face one must be able to love the meanest of creation as oneself.'[5]

Vivekananda and Gandhi never met. Their material lives were on completely independent, unrelated trajectories. And yet it appears that both were nurtured by the same spirit, engaged in a bold and intense exploration to reach broadly similar conclusions. Gandhi's statement above will be rejected by many as being undoable for ordinary mortals caught in the coils of afflictive emotions. What such a critique overlooks, or even denies, is the importance of firstly accepting the ideal and then striving to come close to it despite failures and disappointments.

~

I am aware that this appeal and the perspective presented here may seem utopian to many. That may be so if your focus is largely or only on the big picture—over which you personally have little or no control. And nothing is easier than looking at that big picture and seeing a dystopia in our future. So I will close by explaining how I was saved from this trap.

In April 1993, just before I plunged fully into

the collected works of Swamiji, I happened to be in Calcutta and spent some time at Belur Math. By some providence, I was granted a meeting with Swami Bhuteshananda, the then President of the Ramakrishna Mission. Knowing that I would be given just a few minutes, I lost no time in any self-introduction and just blurted out my anxiety.

'I feel we live in the worst of times. How is one to live in this painful time?' I asked.

Swami Bhuteshananda smiled slightly and said in Hindi:

'Kaal achha ya bura nahin hota. Jeevan har kaal mein sangram hai. Sawaal yeh nahin hota ki doosre kya kar rahe hain. Hamein sirf yeh dekhna hai ki hum kya karsakte hain, kya kar rahe hain.'

('Time is never good nor bad. For life in all times is a noble struggle. The question is not what others are doing. All that matters is what we can do, what we are doing.')

This advice shaped much more than the series of articles on Vivekananda, which I wrote in the following months. The gravity of confidence behind Swami Bhuteshananda's words opened spaces within, it lessened the domination of fear within. This advice can be a fair wind in the sails of anyone journeying from fear to love. It is only then that we might be able to see beyond the surface. Looking beneath, we might find that the hatred and resentment roiling on the surface is actually fear and a desperate vulnerability.

This is why Swami Vivekananda urges us to be heroes and equates sturdy 'manliness' with the overcoming of afflictive emotions. 'Never can hatred and malice vanish from one's heart unless one becomes a hero, and unless one is free from these, how can one become truly civilised?'[6]

But the freedom and heroism that Swamiji is referring to may not be possible without at least an appreciation, if not acceptance, of the metaphysics which anchored his deep confidence that each one of us has the potential to be free. His logic is impeccable.

One: everything in time, space and causation is bound.

Two: but the soul is beyond all time, all space, all causation.

It is nature that is bound, not the soul.

Therefore, he reasoned: '...proclaim your freedom and be what you are—ever free, ever blessed.'[7]

Those who are not comfortable with or don't believe in a 'soul' could consider replacing the term with having faith in yourself. As Swamiji says elsewhere:

'The Vedanta teaches men to have faith in themselves first. As certain religions of the world say that a man who does not believe in a personal God outside of himself is an atheist, so the Vedanta says, a man who does not believe in himself is an atheist.'[8]

Each one of us has to choose. Do we see the other's vulnerability in combative terms, as a weak point to strike? Or do we approach the other with the possibility of a shared quest for freedom from fear? It does not matter on what levels of public life and political competition this may or may not be possible. As individuals and as groups within the samaj, we are all free to strive for this freedom.

Acknowledgements

The journey of discovering Swami Vivekananda's life and world would never have begun if not for my friend Anand Bapat. For imbuing this journey with wit, laughter and challenge, I will always remain grateful to Anand and honour his memory.

By agreeing to publish the series I set out to write, Darryl D'Monte gave me an anchor and a focus, which ensured that I did not get lost within the volumes of Swamiji's collected works.

Thanks to the Other India Press, Goa for first publishing Parts I and II.

The essay in section III is written by me but the processes and strivings it attempts to share have been a collective exercise with many friends and fellow travellers. For their fellowship, in often painful soul-searching, I feel a gratitude that cannot adequately be conveyed. Above all, the blessing of this fellowship is celebrated through our shared joy in knowing that *'hari se bada hari ka naam'*.

Notes

Introduction

1   Govind Krishnan V., *Vivekananda: The Philosopher of Freedom* (New Delhi: Aleph Book Company, 2023), p. 147
2   Ibid, p. 150
3   Ibid, p. 172
4   *The Complete Works of Swami Vivekananda, Volume V,* (Calcutta: Advaita Ashram, 1959), p. 92
5   For further reading, the scholars that Medhananda mentions in this context are:

> Ankur Barua. 'The Hindu Cosmopolitanism of Sister Nivedita (Margaret Elizabeth Noble): An Irish Self in Imperial Currents'. *Harvard Theological Review* 113, no. 1, (January 2020): 1-23. https://doi.org/10.1017/S0017816019000324
>
> Brian Hatcher. 'Contemporary Hindu Thought'. *Contemporary Hinduism*, edited by Robin Rinehart, 179-211. Santa Barbara, CA: ABC Clio, 2004
>
> James Madaio. 'Rethinking Neo-Vedanta: Swami Vivekananda and the Selective Historiography of Advaita Vendanta'. *Religions* 8, no. 6, (May 2017):1-12. https://doi.org/10.3390/rel8060101
>
> Jonardon Ganeri. 'Freedom in Thinking: The immersive Cosmopolitanism of Krishnachandra

Bhattacharyya'. *The Oxford Handbook of Indian Philosophy*, edited by Jonardon Ganeri, 718-36. New York: Oxford University Press, 2017

Nalini Bhushan and Jay L. Garfield. *Minds Without Fear: Philosophy in the Indian Renaissance*. New York: Oxford University Press, 2017

Swami Medhanana. 'Asminnasya ca tadyogam sasti: Swami Vivekananda's Interpretation of Brahmasutra 1.1.19 as a Hermeneutic Basis for Samnvayi Vedanta'. *Swami Vivekananda: His Life, Legacy, and Liberative Ethics*, edited by Rita Sherma, 9-28. Lanham, MD: Rowman & Littlefield, 2020.

Swami Medhananda, 'Was Swami Vivekananda a Hindu Supremacist? Revisiting a Long-Standing Debate.' *Religions* 11, no. 7, (July 2020): 1-28.

6 From *The Complete Works of Swami Vivekananda, Volume III*, p. 270-271; qtd. in Swami Medhananda, *Swami Viveknanda's Vedāntic Cosmopolitanism* (New York: Oxford University Press, 2022), p. 5

Part II

1 *The Complete Works of Sister Nivedita, Volume I*, (Calcutta: Advaita Ashram), p. 41.

2 *The Complete Works of Swami Vivekananda, Volume VII*, (Calcutta: Advaita Ashram), p. 60.

3 Ibid, p. 59

4 *The Life of Swami Vivekananda by His Eastern and Western Disciples, Volume I*, (Calcutta: Advaita Ashram), p. 360.

5   Ibid, p. 364-65
6   *The Complete Works of Swami Vivekananda, Volume III,* (Calcutta: Advaita Ashram), p. 373.
7   Ibid, p. 378.
8   Ibid, p. 379
9   *The Complete Works of Swami Vivekananda, Volume II,* (Calcutta: Advaita Ashram, 1958), p. 374.
10 *The Complete Works of Sister Nivedita, Volume 1,* (Calcutta: Advaita Ashram), p. 46.
11 *The Complete Works of Swami Vivekananda, Volume IV,* (Calcutta: Advaita Ashram), p. 159.
12 *The Life of Swami Vivekananda by His Eastern and Western Disciples, Volume II,* (Calcutta: Advaita Ashram), p. 333.
13 *The Complete Works of Sister Nivedita, Volume I,* (Calcutta: Advaita Ashram), p. 48.
14 *The Complete Works of Swami Vivekananda, Volume IV,* (Calcutta: Advaita Ashram), p. 76.

Part III

1   Ramchandra Guha, 'A Father Betrayed', *The Guardian,* Accessed November 2023. https://www.theguardian.com/world/2007/aug/14/india.features111
2   S. Gopalakrishnan, 'Tagore on Nationalism: In Conversation with Prof. Ashis Nandy', *Sahapedia,* Accessed November 2023. https://www.sahapedia.org/tagore-nationalism-conversation-prof-ashis-nandy
3   *The Complete Works of Sister Nivedita, Volume V,* (Calcutta: Advaita Ashram), p. 15

4 Swami Medhananda, *Swami Viveknanda's Vedāntic Cosmopolitanism* (New York: Oxford University Press, 2022), p. 27 in Kindle edition]

5 M. K. Gandhi, *The Story of My Experiments with Truth: An Autobiography* (New Delhi: Om Books International, 2010), p. 370-71

6 *The Complete Works of Swami Vivekananda, Volume VII,* (Calcutta: Advaita Ashram), p. 271

7 *The Complete Works of Swami Vivekananda, Volume VI,* (Calcutta: Advaita Ashram), p. 92-93

8 *The Complete Works of Swami Vivekananda, Volume II,* (Calcutta: Advaita Ashram), p. 294; 'Militating against the dominant view that his philosophy follows Sankara's Advaita Vedanta in all or most of its essentials, I contend that Vivekananda, under the influence of Ramakrishna, reconceived Advaita Vedanta as a nonsectarian, world-affirming, and ethically oriented philosophy. According to my reconstruction, Vivekananda, in contrast to Sankara held that (1) the impersonal Brahman and the personal Sakti are equally real aspects of one and the same Infinite Divine Reality; (2) the universe is a real manifestation of Sakti; (3) since we are all living manifestations of God, we should make Vedanta practical by loving and serving human beings in a spirit of worship; and (4) each of the four Yogas (i.e., basic forms of spiritual practice)—Bhakti-Yoga, Jnana-Yoga, Karma-Yoga, and Raja-Yoga—is a direct and independent path to salvation. Vivekananda also criticized the 'text torturing' of traditional scriptural commentators like Sankara and Ramanuja, anchoring his own Integral Advaita philosophy in a subtle

reinterpretation of the Upanisads, the Bhagavad-Gita, and the Brahmasutra.'—Swami Medhananda, *Swami Viveknanda's Vedāntic Cosmopolitanism* (New York: Oxford University Press, 2022), p. 8.

9 789354 477270